Eight to Sixteen,
an Interval of Time

A Memoir of a Small part of my Life

Martin,

Kevin has told
he of our friendship,
and mutual respect, and
he feels you may enjoy
reading about this long ago
part of my life.

My kind regards,

Ro. Moore

17.02.12

Eight to Sixteen, an Interval of Time

A Memoir of a Small part of my Life

RONALD G. MOORE

© Ronald G. Moore, 2012

Published by Mr Ronald George Moore

A CIP catalogue record for this book is available from the British Library.

ISBN 978-0-9571426-0-2

Book design by Clare Brayshaw

Prepared and printed by:

York Publishing Services Ltd
64 Hallfield Road
Layerthorpe
York YO31 7ZQ

Tel: 01904 431213

Website: www.yps-publishing.co.uk

Dedication

To my dad, there were so many years lost, to my wife Mary, she helped me through the first years of our marriage when I was still traumatised by the passing of my father, my children, and grandchildren, they have given my wife, and I so much pleasure over the years. God Bless them.

Contents

Prologue

When some years ago I mooted the idea of compiling a record of my life between the outbreak of World War 2, and the completion of my formal education, the idea was to research that period thoroughly, however, during the ensuing years, I have recalled events to my family, and in particular my grandchildren, which have been received sometimes with amusement, but often with incredulity, this set me thinking that perhaps this was the wrong approach.

The decision now, is to write an autobiographical account, based on memories only, after all, when most people look back over their lives, and in particular their childhood, they only have memories of events that have had some influence on their lives, some happy, some sad, but all having some profound, and lasting effect.

For reasons that will become obvious as the narrative unfolds, I am covering the year prior to the outbreak of hostilities, this in many ways was the happiest of years, with all the family together, and as it turns out the saddest, up until July. 1946, when I completed my time at Portsmouth Southern Grammar School for Boys, when I first joined, it was known as a Secondary, but later changed it's name, in those days Portsmouth had two Secondary's for boys, two for girls, and Portsmouth Grammar School for Boys, it was not until much later that girls were allowed to attend, such luxuries!! When I left that July it was to be the start of my training as a Joiner, and Cabinet Maker in H.M. Dockyard, Portsmouth.

I would like to recall my very earliest memory, of particular interest to my own children. It was my third birthday, and the family at that time only consisted of myself, and my brother Edward who was approaching one year old. We had been summoned to my uncle Sid's to collect my birthday present, a very large Encylopaedia, not wrapped, but just in a paper bag, this I had great difficulty in lifting from the floor. That volume still exists to this day, although in a rather a tattered state after so much use over the years by myself, and my family.

I have no doubt, that as this text unfolds, there will be slight historical inaccuracy's, however, I hope that any of my contemporaries reading this, will forgive me.

CHAPTER 1

The Family

February 1939, the family consisted of mum, dad, and six children, four boys, and two girls, I was the eldest, being born 20.10.30. Our home was a small two up two down terraced house situated at the bottom of a narrow alley running between The Victory public house, and Smeeds the off-license on the north side of Highland road in Southsea, Portsmouth. The pub was known locally as The Gravediggers, because of it's location opposite the cemetery, years later, following a refurbishment it was decided to change the name, and, a public debate decided on The Diggers, that went up on the sign, a compromise as it turns out, because it was felt The Gravediggers was a little disrespectful, today though, that is the name on the sign, whatever happened to respect!!

As I have said the house was small, particularly for such a large family, but we seemed to manage, as young children we probably thought it was great fun sleeping several to a bed, us four boys slept in a double iron bedstead, and the two girls were with mum, and dad in the other room, the only saving grace of so many being in one room was that it helped in the cold weather, no central heating in those far off days just blankets, and quilts, the duvets of the day. The front door was panelled with a clear glass fanlight over, I mention this because it has some significance which I will tell you of later, this opened on to a long narrow passage, just inside the door to the left at the high level was a coin operated gas meter taking old pennies, and, the only way to feed this when the gas ran out, was to stand on a chair, insert the coins, and twist the key until the coins fell into the pan at the bottom. The passage ran from the front door to the scullery/kitchen at the rear, the front room was the first on the right, the narrow staircase to the two bedrooms went up between two walls, and beyond that on the right was the dining cum living room. The front room was only used on very special occasions, but the living room was the most used area of the house, we ate, talked, and played here. The lavatory was at the back of the house, but I cannot remember whether it was in the yard, or connected to the house with a door from the scullery, I can, in my mind see quite clearly the thick wooden seat going from wall to wall with the hole in the centre, the high level water tank, complete with chain to pull when flushing, and the squares of newspaper on a loop of string hung on a nail, no soft toilet tissues in those days, and it always seemed cold, and damp, not a place to hang about in winter.

I can remember very little about the furnishings, the floors were covered in lino, and rugs, the staircase had a narrow cord runner, the walls were clad in wallpaper, but what the colour of that or the paintwork I have no idea. In the living room the table had a chenille cloth covering what must have been a polished top, but I do not know, on one wall hung a crumb tray complete with a curved brush, recently this very useful tool is making a come back. On the wall adjacent the door hung a silk embroidered picture commemorating an uprising in the far east, my father as a serving Royal Marine was involved in quelling that conflict, no one in the family seems to know what happened to that wonderful piece of work, all the furniture was stored for a good part of the war so perhaps it was lost in one of the many moves in the years that followed. The scullery, or kitchen as it would now be called, had a deep Butler type sink bowl with cold running water, a table, and chairs, and in the corner, a "copper" for boiling the white linen. The construction of this was concrete with an inner lining of galvanised steel, a tin lid with a wooden handle, and a fire grate under, to operate, the copper had to be hand filled with cold water, the fire lit under, and then it was a matter of waiting until the water came to the boil, add the washing powder, and the linen. When the process was complete, the sheets had to be lifted out with a copper stick, a round piece of beech about eighteen inches long. into a small galvanised bath, and into the sink for rinsing under the cold tap. Once this was complete the washing was wrung by hand, and transferred to the back yard where it was put through the "mangle", this consisted of a cast iron stand, two large rollers at the top with a screw above to set the space between them, to one side a large wheel with a wooden handle which enabled the rollers to be turned, under the rollers was a tray with a lip to allow the water to be caught in a bucket placed under. This whole procedure was arduous in the extreme, but mothers seemed to cope in those days, sometimes not too well I suspect, particularly in the winter, when the washing had to be dried indoors on a wooden clothes horse, mum seemed to take it all in her stride, most women's aspirations in those days were not great, just as well things have moved on.

Looking back it was quite a harsh life, but of course we did not know any different, us boys were all dressed mostly the same, course shirts, short trousers, long socks, and boots, the girls I rather think had dresses, and cardigans, in 1938 there was only Daphne, Sheila did not arrive until early the following year, one thing for sure, we were very happy, helped by the fact that dad was to be around from then on.

CHAPTER 2

The House, and Around

The three piece suite in the front room was covered in rexine (vinyl), very few soft covers in those days, hard wearing, but not very comfortable, some families had these for the whole of their married lives. Communication with the outside world was through the daily newspapers, some of those titles still exist to this day, and the wireless (radio), very few ordinary families, no lack of respect meant, had telephones, so letter writing was the order of the day if you needed to contact relatives living some way away, if only we did that more often these days. The wireless was I believe an Echo, it had straight sides, and a semi circular top, and powered by accumulators, these resembled small car batteries with clear glass complete with carrying handle, two were necessary to run the wireless, so you always had to have four to hand, two of which were always on charge at the local shop, in this instance a sweet shop! You can imagine, regular trips had to made to swap the batteries when one set ran out of power, I can remember having to do this on many an occasion. The wireless of this era invariably had short wave facility, very useful if, like my father you were a boxing enthusiast, he could then tune in to live broadcasts coming from anywhere in the world, more often than not, in the middle of the night.

There is I suppose, very little to be said of the house, particularly in those austere days when children did not have their own rooms, complete with CD players, TV etc. The garden however, was a haven, which ran from the front of the house to the rear of the off-license on the main road, it must have been about 100 metres in length. Close to the house in one corner was a huge pear tree, this bore so much fruit that it was impossible to consume the whole crop, the bottom third of the garden was taken up with fruit bushes, logan berries, and gooseberries, the round fat hairy variety which always seemed so sweet when eaten. These bushes caused us children a whole lot of trouble getting at the fruit because of the thorns, until father cut a series of paths through them, this also gave us greater scope as a play area. The space between the pear tree, and the fruit bushes was a football pitch, cricket pitch, or whatever we wanted to make of it, in those days you had to make your own entertainment, that was quite easy in fact because we did not know any different.

What of the area around the house, it was situated at the bottom of an alleyway between what was then, the Victory Public House, and Smeeds the off licence. White Cloud Place, the two blocks of cottages on each side of this were White Cloud Cottages, our's was on the right hand side No 2. Next to the off licence was the sweet shop/tobacconist, this had on the counter the obligatory Vantas bottle, a large clear glass round container complete with a tap, the liquid inside was I believe, carbonated water, and was sold as a drink for a halfpenny a glass, old money. Adjacent to these shops was a store house owned by Parkes the removal company, this had a large cellar under with access from the street by means of two large cellar flaps, this had a very important use during the war years, more of that later.

The shop on the corner of Highland Road, and Winter Road was Eaton's the butcher, I was a frequent visitor to collect the family meat ration, often you were not sure what you would get until you arrived there, and had to take what was available. Arthur Senior, and his wife befriended me, and this allowed me to become great pal's with their son Arthur Junior, he was the same age as myself, strangely I do not recall him at school. They were good people, and often included me in their outings, even to the Hippodrome theatre, ours was such a large family this would have been out of the question. Opposite the butchers on the corner was the bakers, and a little further down among quite a few small shops, was Osborne's.

the grocer, here I remember they always had a large display of biscuits in glass topped tins, these were on a rack in front of the counter at an angle so that you could easily see the contents, some had broken biscuits which were sold off cheap, always popular with us children.

Adjacent to the pub on other side from White Cloud Place was a terrace of tiny cottages running at an angle to the main road, these had long narrow front gardens terminating at a path to one side of the church, these were always well kept, and because these properties were at a lower level than those around them, you looked down on them, giving the impression that you were viewing a separate village. Looking down on that area today, nothing has changed, the gardens are still all well kept with wonderful floral displays to delight the passer by.

The high church off St. Margaret's where I attended for choir, cubs etc. I will cover later.

Two other shops are worth a mention, both further east along Highland Road towards Eastney Barracks, one was Butlers cycles, still there to this day trading under the same name, and a cooked meat shop, selling hot food as well as cold, sausages, faggots, mushy peas, and the like. You went along with your own basin to collect the goodies, I invariably went with my dad,, that wonderful smell is still with me today.

Another building of note, was the Odeon cinema on the corner of Festing Grove, only completed a few years before the war, and a premier "picture house" in Portsmouth, I cannot in all honesty, remember having been there, rather too grand I suspect, the Regal at Eastney was more the mark, known locally as the "bug hutch". Here on Saturday afternoons we would vent our feelings at the site, and sounds of The Lone Ranger, Laurel and Hardy etc. all for two pence, and if you were lucky, you would be given another penny to buy a triangular Wall's ice lolly, or whatever they were called in those far off days.

CHAPTER 3

Interests

School was only a few streets away, Reginald Road, I cannot recall too much of my time there, and often wonder why, perhaps like most children I could not wait to get home, and play. I do remember that I followed the football team. and that I watched them play in the school finals at Fratton Park, the home of Portsmouth Football Club one year, a large effigy called Reggie was taken along to help our team on the field, I cannot remember what the result was, I suspect that we lost, I may well have remembered had we won. One teacher only stands out in my mind, "pop" Williams, our form master, he always appeared to wear ginger plus four suits, plus fours being the trousers which were banded below the knees, and worn with long wooley socks, and heavy shoes. He would cane us for the slightest wrongdoing, in those days of course, corporal punishment was rife, even encouraged, and consisted of you holding your hand out with the palm uppermost, and being whacked on the palm with a flexible cane, often many times, very painful and probably inflicting injuries at times, not such happy school days.

Out of school the family led a very congenial, and happy life, we always ate well, and were always clean, and tidy, mother always maintained, like many of her generation, that soap, and water cost nothing, not quite true, but you will understand what she meant. Mum, and dad were very proud of their family, this was shown at its best when the whole family went out together. There were some regular places we visited, one was Sunday church parade at Eastney Barracks, dad would be in his uniform complete with small silver topped cane held under one arm, I believe this was only allowed when they walked out in uniform on special occasions, these days no serviceman walks out in uniform, partly for security reasons, but more often than not because theirs is very much a day job which necessitates the wearing of a uniform, and only too glad to take it off before they depart for home at the end of the day. On the occasion of these visits we would listen to the band, and watch the marching display, and sometimes would be invited into the officers mess, they were unforgettable days, I am still moved by the sight, and sound of the"Royals". That officers mess now houses the Royal Marine Museum, and is in my opinion one of the finest military museums in the country, if not the finest, I am of course a little biased. During my latter working years, I was very much involved with the furnishing work there, something which is very ongoing as the museum expands.

Another family outing I vividly recall was to the locks at Eastney. We would walk along Highland Road, and Henderson Road, past the old pumping station, into Ferry Road to a point where the ferry plies back, and forth to Haying Island. The latter section of this road stands on a promontory with water at each side, the Eastney Lakeside had a small beach area with many small boats anchored off the shore, on the other side was Langston Channel forming the waterway between Portsmouth, and Hayling Island. After spending time watching the boats we would make our way back to Eastney Road, go north for a while, then turn into Locksway Road, finally reaching Longshore Way. a section of the shoreline overlooking the harbour, complete with a beach, anchored boats, and a pub, where in the summer we all sat outside, enjoying our lemonade, and crisps, "Smiths" of course because they were made locally. This area is still very much as it was in those days, and although not visiting socially these days, while at work was often involved in the refurbishment of that pub, "The Thatched House", I daresay had my father been here today, he would still have liked to partake of a drink in that watering hole, he liked a drink, but not in excess.

While on this point I must tell you of a related incident which I have never spoken of previously to anyone, you will remember my reference to the pub on the corner of the alley leading down to our cottage, they had a gypsy band, one tune they always seemed to be playing, and still haunts me to this day, "O Play to me Gypsy". This particular night I woke up, and called out to mother, for what, I do not know, there was no answer so I went down stairs, neither my mother nor my father could be found anywhere. I went along to the front door, climbed the panelling by holding on to the pipe leading to the gas meter, this enabled me to look through the fanlight over the door, the pub was not too far away, and I could hear the strains of the band playing, that is where my parents were, "Home Alone" you see is not a new phenomenon!!

As children, life centred around going to school, coming home to play, eating, and sleeping, a routine which could be relied upon to ensure a very stable home life, sometimes- and only rarely, this gets shaken by some trauma, and this happened when my younger sister Sheila, then only about three months old developed bronchial pneumonia, and was rushed to the old Royal Hospital, no longer there, I did not fully understand how serious this was at the time only that my parents were worried about the possible outcome, mother cried a great deal, but in the end all was well, and she fully recovered from her ordeal, and never suffered any ill effects. She was mum's favourite child for always, and although she was the youngest of us she was the first to be taken from us through cancer, thankfully mother had passed on a couple of years before, I know she would have had great difficulty in dealing with that.

How was my own time taken up outside of school? My father being a serving Royal Marine, it was inevitable that he would wish me to join the Royal Marine Cadet Force, and this I did. The uniform was almost identical to it's senior counterpart, except that the trousers were cut off just below the knee, and from there down to the boots were "putties", a navy blue wide bandage wound around the legs, a legacy of the 14/18 war, one other item was different, was the sam brown type belt complete with brass buckles, something normally only worn by officers. You can imagine, when we paraded at Eastney Barracks we would all be turned out impeccably thanks to our fathers, they taking as much pride in our uniforms as they would have done their own.

The junior corp had it's own band, and "Field Gun Crew" neither of which I belonged to, I was part if the infantry, carrying out all the drill movements as seen being carried out by the Royals. I was certainly too small to be a member of the gun crew, in fact I did not start to grow too much until I was about fifteen years old, this in fact did not deter me, I enjoyed travelling around giving displays, and supporting the gun crew when in competition with the local establishments. Following the outbreak of the war, the force was disbanded, but when hostilities were over, was reformed, and is going strong to this day.

My other prime interest was singing, in a choir that is at St. Margaret's church not two minutes away from our cottage. The vicar at that time was a Rev. Duke-Baker, a rather distant person, only speaking to you through his curate Father Copley. a wonderful man who later became an essential prop for the family. I am sure that in those days I was not a true believer, I loved to sing at any occasion whether it was Matins, Evensong, Weddings, or Funerals, and I would be paid for it! For normal services it would be a halfpenny, for funerals a penny, and weddings two pence, what wealth.

The Canoe Lake was only about ten minutes walk away from where I lived, and the activities on, and around the lake occupied a great deal of my time during the summer months, sometimes as a family we would go there, and perhaps be taken out in a rowing boat, they were the long sleek hulled variety with ample room for all of us. At other times I would go there with my friends or my brother to fish for crabs, fish heads would be collected from the local fishmonger, supplied free, probably glad to get rid of them. these were tied to a length of string, and lowered into the edge of the lake. great fun because we would always have plenty of bites. I recall that at one time someone in the family, not my father, made me a boat of plywood, complete with a deck, and superstructure, at the time it seemed enormous, but was probably only a couple of feet long. As you can imagine, this vessel made many trips to the lake, and in many differing forms, I will explain, I was not aware of it at the time, but I was obviously interested in woodwork, and would often alter the vessel, at one time all that was left of it was the hollow hull with no deck, this proved a great attraction to all the children who gathered around, because the crabs caught were deposited in the hull full of water, and towed around the perimeter of the lake, those summer days always seemed endless.

Very little has been said of my brothers, and sisters, I can only imagine that they were for the most part too young with the exception of Ed, to be involved in any of my activities, my only real memories of them were the outings as a family. I often wondered why my brothers name was shortened to Ed, it was not until years later when he took up his career in the Royal Navy that his colleagues called him Ted, that has stuck with everyone except his original family, to us he is still Ed.

My mother, and father always appeared tall to me, my father was of course, but mum was quite short, however she was slim in those days, we were all so young that they appeared taller I suppose. Mother came from a family of twelve children, and dad was one of fourteen, unheard of in this day, and age, of that considerable family, the ones I knew could be counted on one hand.

CHAPTER 4

A Little of My Dad

Father joined the Royal Marines at fourteen years old during the first world war. and mother always insisted that he served on a warship at the battle of Jutland, but the facts do not quite add up, unless of course he advanced his age, not uncommon at the time, one thing is certain, and that is, that he did serve his country during that conflict. From then on he served in many ships, only one springs to mind, the mighty battleship H.M.S. Nelson. I can remember her shape as though I was looking at her now. Her superstructure was towards the aft, one funnel, two sixteen inch gun turrets forward, each with three barrels, and an identical turret aft, a most formidable fighting machine. Never one for promotion, dad preferred, as many men did in those days, to remain on the "lower deck", he kept his nose clean so to speak, eventually gaining three good conduct stripes, and his marksman's badge, achieved as a fine shot with the old Lee Enfield 303 rifle.

Very little was seen of dad during the period between the wars, because commissions in those days were between two, and a half, to three years duration, often on the other side of the world, on those long trips he would carry out laundry work for some of the officers to earn extra money for when he came home. At certain ports of call, it was customary for the ships company to entertain the local dignitaries, the Marine Band was always involved of course, but various other acts were gathered from the ratings themselves, my father among them, it would appear that he was quite an accomplished tap dancer!

The reason for dad being home based for so long prior to the outbreak of world war two, was that he was approaching retirement, and was posted to Eastney Barracks to complete his time, almost a day job, this allowed me as the eldest son to get to know my father for the very first time in my life. After twenty two years unblemished service, all ratings were awarded a good conduct medal together with a gratuity of twenty pounds, an absolute fortune then, needless to say when dad received his, we were all treated to something special, mine was a bike, I had coveted owning one for as long as I could remember, it was a Raleigh, one of those with the distinctive concave embellishments to the top of the forks, bought at Butlers in Eastney, and I suspect on hire purchase, the only thing was that I could not ride it because of the size, almost too small for dad, but allowed for me to grow into, parents still do this to this day, the pleasure of receiving was somewhat diminished in these circumstances, the thought was there though.

That year prior to the war was quite idyllic, the whole family together as never before, enjoying experiences which in my case were perhaps a little late, never mind, they are thankfully ingrained in the memory for ever. One of those was a visit to Guernsey in the channel islands, while my father was on one of his ships goodwill visits he became friendly with a local family, who invited us out to the island for a holiday, I experienced a sea trip for the first time, overnight as I recall, not very pleasant, many of those on board were ill with sea sickness. I have only two memories of that visit, one was a family picnic, to the countryside in a cart drawn by horses, and a visit to the tiny shell covered church, which I believe is the smallest in the world.

I must backtrack a little now, and hope you will forgive me, but a couple of things have happened lately that have jogged my memory about our cottage. I heard someone on the radio referring to the old six inch wax records, and it reminded me of the record player my parents had, a cabinet standing on four legs with a turntable at the top enclosed with a lid, under the turntable was a cupboard for stowage of the records, winding handle, and needles. The unit was charged by inserting the handle into the side of the cabinet, and winding, after the record was placed on the turntable the arm with the steel needle in place was lowered on to the record following the pushing of the start lever. This particular model did not have the familiar trumpet to enhance the sound, probably just as well because the reproduction was not too good, what records we had I have no idea, I doubt that I was interested in the popular music of the time. Another memory was brought about by seeing a vividly decorated chamber pot in a shop window, now used as a plant pot, or whatever you wished to make of it, but in those days before the war, and perhaps in some bedrooms today, there, under the bed was the "po" in case nature called during the night, sometimes the smell of urine at the top of our cottage on awaking in the morning was quite unpleasant.

Although unaware of it in 1938, the possibility of war was there at least two years before, and when it did happen in early September 1939 I really did not understand what the full impact would be, I was though very soon, with devastating effect.

CHAPTER 5

The Storm Following the Calm

Although not aware of the build-up to the declaration of war, I do remember the speech delivered over the radio by the then prime minister, Neville Chamberlain which proclaimed, "we are now at war with Germany", the date September 3rd 1939. I am sure that my mother believed dad would remain a member of staff at Eastney Barracks, but that was not to be, and he was duly notified that he would be drafted to the battleship H.M.S. Royal Oak.

As was customary in those days when a ship was recommisioned, the ships company would march from their base to the berth in Portsmouth Dockyard, almost always with the Royal Marine Band leading the way, I cannot recall the exact date that my father actually joined his ship, or in fact whether he caught a train from the harbour station, and joined it somewhere else, but it was soon after the outbreak of the war. Eastney Barracks was situated in Cromwell Road, and on the day of his departure all the family gathered on the corner of Eastney Street, and Cromwell Road to obtain a good view of the company as they left their base, there was no band on this occasion, and as they came through the main gate they turned right, and marched towards us.

There is nothing to quite compare with a company of Marines on the march, their navy blue uniforms complete with highly polished buttons, and badges, white pith helmets, and belts, and of course highly polished boots, a highly charged, and emotional occasion at any time, but now, nobody had any idea how long it would be before this fine body of men would return home again. At last dad came into view, and we all waved him goodbye, he could not acknowledge us, but we all knew that he had seen us, they marched to Highland Road, crossed over the road to the main bus station to catch the transport which would carry them to the harbour, to board his ship or to catch a train north, I did not know, from what happened later I do know that the Royal Oak was to be anchored in Scapa Flow sound North of Scotland. Very little changed for a while, and although dad was away again, life went on very much as it had always done.

The mode of public transport throughout the city of Portsmouth at this time was the trolley bus, the old tram system had been removed some years before, they of course ran on steel rails, and driven by electricity drawn from an overhead cable by means of a spring loaded pole with a pulley at the end which located the overhead cable, they were very noisy, but I rather think, much loved by the public at large. The trolley buses had conventional tyred wheels, were also driven by electricity, but had two poles, these I remember would often come adrift from the cables, the bus would stop, and the conductor would leap from the platform, pull a long pole from under the bodywork at the rear of the veyicle, and proceed to replace the pulley wheels on to the cables, not an easy task.

Very few families had cars at this time, but many had bicycles. The main employer in Portsmouth was H.M. Dockyard with probably between 25000, and 30000 workmen of every possible trade, most of which rode cycles. When the hooter sounded at the end of the working day it was a mass exodus through all the gates around the perimeter wall, every road from the "yard" was completely blocked for about ten minutes, and then all was quiet again.

Changes were inevitably taking place, some more obvious than others, but all to be with us for a very long time. The threat of air raids made a priority of a complete blackout at night, all windows had heavy curtains or inner curtain linings of dense black material, and everyone was encouraged to adhere tape diagonally both ways on all panes of glass to minimise splintering in the event of a bomb blast, and all vehicles had shades over the top of their head lights so that from above no light could be seen.

Munitions factories now worked round the clock, and because of the shortage of iron ore, all railings, gates etc. were commandeered to help the shortfall, oddly enough much of these were never used, and at the end of the war were re-instated. Ration books were issued to all members of the public, young, and old, and covered essential items of food, and clothing, some things were not rationed such as fruit, although these were difficult to come by, and some, such as bananas were rarely seen. Offal was not considered part of *the* meat ration, and this is where our friends the Eaton's helped out on many an occasion. I would have to go to their shop just before closing time when very few people were about, and Arthur senior would disappear into the rear of the premises, and come out with a small white bag containing liver, kidneys, and the like, I would quickly hide the hag in my pocket, and run off home. In those days if word got out that the butcher had offal, a queue would soon form in the street, in fact, queuing was to become a way of life from then on.

Another major change, was the erection of air raid shelters, or Anderson Shelters, every family had one in their garden, they were of corrugated iron construction, only about eight feet by six feet, the sides were verticle, and the whole roof was semi circular, one end was blanked off, the other had a small access to allow entry, inside was just enough headroom to stand. The whole was buried in the ground about four feet, and a good layer of earth covered the top as added protection. These shelters proved very successful except in the event of a direct hit by a bomb, then thankfully those inside knew nothing. Soon these shelters became an extension of the home, fitted out with bunks, decorated, and complete with a door to keep out the draft, the floor was more often than not a duck board, essential because in a heavy rainfall several inches of water would form on the floor, these shelters were also prone to condensation running down the walls, inevitable with so many of the family in occupation. Our neighbour I remember built a timber shelter on the outside of the opening consisting of two sides, a roof, and a bench seat, this was his own little cubby hole where he, and sometimes me would sit, and watch the air raids during the night, I still cannot understand why my mother allowed me to do this, I suppose it eased the cramped conditions inside. I know that I felt very grown up with no thought for the possible danger of flying shrapnel. Once the air raids, signalled by an intermittent hooter, became more frequent, the whole family would be put to bed each night in the shelter to eliminate the frantic dash to the shelter should the alarm be sounded during the night.

You will remember I previously mentioned that the furniture store next to the butcher had a large cellar, this was completely emptied, and converted to a public air raid shelter, opened whenever a raid was signalled. On several occasions the family went there overnight, I have no idea why, perhaps sometimes my mother felt lonely, and had a need for some company, I do know that I did not like it at all, I felt that I was not the big brother of the family among so many people, most of which I did not know. One particular thing I disliked was the communal sleeping, that dislike of "communal living" was to stay with me for the rest of my life, and, although on numerous occasions in the future I would have to live in this way, the aversion never left me.

Everyone including babes in arms were issued with gas masks, gas attacks were feared by the authorities, rightly so because of the experiences of the troops in France during the first world war, as it happens those fears were to be proved unfounded. The grownups, and the childrens gas masks were made of a black rubber based compound with a clear plastic visor, this covered the whole face, and was held in place with wide adjustable straps around the back of the head, in the front, covering the mouth, and nose was what looked like a bean tin with a screw in filter. This hideous piece of equipment was kept in a cardboard box complete with a length of cord to enable you to sling it across your shoulder, whenever you went out you were expected to carry it with you. Part of the routine at school was to have gas alert practise, this entailed putting on the gas mask for about half an hour while still carrying out the lesson. The babes in arms had what rather looked like a carry cot with a see through cover to the top as a "gas mask" how secure this would have been I have no idea, just as well they were never brought into use.

The inevitability of war was known a month or so before the negotiations finally broke down, and rehearsals were often carried out for the evacuation of mothers, and their children to safe area's in the country and on these occasions we would have to pack our bags, put on our coats, and hats, and sling our gas masks, then report to a designated area usually the school, it will be worth noting that only those who had expressed a desire to be evacuated would be required to carry out this routine. Actual evacuation began soon after the outbreak of war, but for many it was to prove far too traumatic, and a very large number returned home after a short stay in the country.

For mum, myself, and my brothers, and sisters it appeared that dad was just away on another commission, he would often write, but there was a difference to the norm in that all his mail was censured, vital in case any seemingly innocent information was passed to the enemy.

Early in October 1939 mum received a letter from dad, and in it was a request for a new gunnery badge for his number one uniform, one made of gold braid. Many Navy Outfitters existed in Portsmouth, but dad would always purchase anything he required in the Arcade off Commercial Road, this was almost entirely of shops catering for the armed forces uniforms, and ancillary items of equipment, this arcade still forms part of the modern Cascade Precinct, but the shop fronts are all of modern design, a great pity, particularly as today there is a revival of the old style polished timber fronts, and that was as they were in those far off days, somewhat like Burlington in London.

The day was October 14th 1939 when the family proceeded to Commercial Road to purchase dad's gunnery badges, I doubt that we went on the trolley bus but probably walked, with my youngest sister Sheila in the pram, and unless we were off school for some reason it must have been a Saturday, I really cannot remember, one thing was very obvious, had mum listened to the news that morning we would not have been in Commercial Road. We entered the naval tailors, and there on the counter was a newspaper, on the front of which was a photograph of my fathers ship with the headlines indicating it had been sunk, she had been anchored in Scapa Flow behind seemingly impenetrable defences, and yet somehow a German "U" boat had managed to get into the sound, and torpedo the Royal Oak. Years later of course, I found out it was in the early hours of Saturday 14.10.39 that the "Oak" was struck with several torpedoes causing the death of 833 of her crew.

I have no idea whether any of the family apart from myself, and mum saw the newspaper or realised the implication of those headlines, I only know that we were stunned by the news, and promptly left the shop in a bewildered silence.

It must have been a dreadful journey home, because mum, and I knew that all we could do when we arrived there was to wait for the telegram from the Admiralty informing mum as to whether dad had survived or not. I now know when it did arrive because I have that telegram, it was the following day, Sunday, and it read:- "Deeply regret to report death of your husband on War service" Marines Portsmouth. Words cannot explain the turmoil of those first few days, mum cried a great deal, so did I, thinking back on those days I believe I was more stunned to think that my dad had been taken from me at a time when most children need them more than ever before, I am sure that I could not take in the fact that I would never see him again, although at that time I had no idea whether his body would be recovered, as it turns out it was not, some were, and were buried on the shore of the sound. The irony was, that had he not carried out one last act of courage he may still be with us today. At the bottom of the alley where we lived, a "U" shaped road existed with each end terminating in Haslemere Road, it was in fact three separate roads St. Ann's, St. Albans, and Tower Road, and one of my dad's shipmates lived in St. Ann's. This shipmates wife later told my mum that dad had reached the guard rail around the upper deck, only to find his friend was missing, he went back to the mess deck and found him, according to the wife they both dived over the side together, I have some doubts about that because had he survived, dad, because of his medical problems would probably not have survived the cold of the sound, but would have been found. Reading about the sinking, I know that at some point a fire ball swept through the marines mess, I hate to think of him caught in that, I will never know, but only pray that however he lost his life it was without pain, I do know that he probably made the ultimate sacrifice to save his friend.

Life went on, but in the knowledge that we would not only have to survive whatever the war had in store for us, but to do it without the prop of my father, who, although would have been away most of the time was always in contact through his letters.

Support, following the loss of my father came from every direction, mum had visits, and I say "visits" because dad's commanding officer Lt. Col. Hunt, and his good lady wife did not just come once to our house, but often, a sign of true concern from someone in such an elevated position, and at such a time. Some years later I was indebted to them for quite another reason, and I will relate that episode when I come to that period. Neighbours did everything possible to ease the burden of those early days, and a mainstay up until our eventual evacuation from Portsmouth was Father Copley, the curate at St. Margaret's.

CHAPTER 6

The End of the Line

Although I attended church on a regular basis, I cannot say with any certainty that I was a devout Christian, not wholly understanding the full implication of the Church of England faith, I certainly did not wonder, as did many grown-ups, why, if a God exists, should he have taken my father away from us so early in his life, I was too young to understand that train of thought, and I carried on attending services at St.Margaret's as I always had done, with just one difference. Father Copley took on the role of father figure, something I accepted quite willingly, and my mother was glad of in the circumstances

Shortages of everything began to bite, somehow we adjusted to this fact, and if anything, thrived, children had certain extras such as man made orange juice to supplement the lack of fresh fruit, and I remember having regular doses of cod liver oil of malt a terrible thick brown sticky substance, which not only tasted vile, but was difficult to swallow, very good for you, so mum said, who was she kidding! The winter was approaching, and the lack of sufficient coal or any kind of fuel for the open fires, and copper was a constant problem, I am sure that a good many of the older generation did not survive because of hypothermia. Mum was a great knitter, just as well, because although wool was difficult to come by, whenever she could obtain any she would beaver away producing jumpers, scarves, and even socks to help keep the family warm.

The air raids became more frequent, only to be expected because of the Naval Base, and ancillary military establishments in, and around Portsmouth. The defences around the island, and surrounding area were formidable, with not only anti-aircraft guns placed strategically at Eastney Barracks, the dockyard, the common at Southsea, churchyards etc but everywhere there were barrage balloons suspended on a wide metal tape, flying, if that is the correct word, at differing heights above the ground, from a few hundred feet, to several thousand feet, they were attached to a large drum on a lorry which would wind them in when they required inflating with hydrogen. The idea was for the metal tape to get caught in the propeller or wings of the incoming enemy aircraft, at night these had some success, but the fighter planes acting as escorts to the bombers often shot them out of the sky, quite spectacular because they would catch fire, and float to the ground sometimes landing on buildings, and catching them alight. As children we would sometimes go during the day to one of the sites where the balloon winch lorries were parked, and watch the balloons being brought back down for refilling with gas. I remember one night during a raid, I was sitting out in the wooden structure adjacent to the entrance to the shelter with our neighbour, when enemy fire shot down a balloon, it immediately caught fire, and fell to earth, well, not quite because it landed on Park's furniture store in Haslemere Road, setting it alight, and illuminating the whole area, it caused a great deal of damage, and must have helped the enemy bombers to light their way to their targets.

All this activity on these night raids gave rise to a new hobby for us children, shrapnel collecting on the following mornings, shrapnel being the splinters of metal from the bombs, and shells fired from the anti aircraft guns, this created competitions between all of us, boys, and girls as to who would find the largest pieces, one of the best sites for collection was at the junction of Highland Road, and Festing Grove, most of this was from the anti-aircraft guns, probably those at Eastney barracks which were aimed to catch the incoming enemy aircraft.

All that had happened, inevitably marred the approach to Christmas that first year of the war, but something quite unexpected occurred. We all hung our socks to the bed rail as usual, expecting the normal supply of an apple, orange, and a few sweets to go with the presents. Looking back on that Christmas I wondered how we expected to get anything in the light of mum's financial state, combined with the shortages of the time, but I suppose we were ever hopeful. The socks had something in them, but I cannot recall what, it was the very large, long white boxes that we all had that so obviously intrigued us. Apparently the Free French people living in England decided to give all war orphans a present, and this was it, a box full of small gifts made up to suit boys, and girls, a wonderful gesture which gave so much pleasure, and did much to help at this most difficult time.

The winter passed, and spring arrived, the improvement in the weather as always making everyone feel a little more hopeful, but not too much so, the news all around was not good, and it looked very much like the war would continue for a very long time. The air raids continued, and each night the family would repair to the shelter, and try to sleep, if we were lucky. on some nights there were no raids, and everyone heaved a sigh of relief, most mornings though we awoke to carnage, houses, and public buildings flattened, great craters in the roads, and much loss of life. Our immediate neighbourhood faired reasonably well, and we did not lose any of our close friends or relatives, but each day us children would go to school, and wonder whether a full compliment would attend. Often because of electricity, water or gas supply being cut off for one reason or another we would not have to attend school, sometimes for some days, this we welcomed, but it did nothing to further our education.

I believe it was during the summer of 1940 that a new period of the war began, daylight raids over the city, this in many ways was much more frightening, being able to see the bombers approaching with their fighter escorts, and then the releasing of their bombs aimed at supposedly military targets, but more often than not dropped indiscriminately. For us children, often in the playground at school, the sight was exhilarating, the danger forgotten when the R.A.F. fighters would come out of the clouds or sun, and begin a "dog fight" with the enemy escort fighters. The

R.A.F. at that period had been supplied with Hurricanes, and Spitfires, what a beautiful aircfraft the latter was, a personal favourite of mine, and remains so to this day. The enemy fighters were no match for our planes, and whenever one of them was shot down we would give a loud cheer, then when we left school for the day we would endeavour to find pieces of the aircraft. All this activity helped to cover up the grief of losing dad, it was not until a long time after that, that the full impact of his loss came home to me, then there would be times when I would wake during the night, and cry to myself, sometimes I would go back to sleep sometimes not, sometimes during the day I would have spells of sullenness, and what must have been depression when the weight of the whole world seemed on my shoulders, it was at these times that I turned to father Copley, on the evenings of choir practice I would have the opportunity to talk with him.

The church was very much a sanctuary in more ways than one, meeting my fellow choir boys, and the ancillary staff, what was left of them following the call-up of all men over the age of eighteen years, that is except those on what was considered to be essential work, and of course father Copley. Talking to them, and more importantly, singing with them was a great release from the stresses then being encountered at home. I gathered from conversations that I overheard between mum. and our curate friend that she hoped that one day I would enter the ministry, but I at no time gave any indication that, that was the path I wished to follow, at that early age I do not believe I had any idea what career to pursue.

A couple of years ago I visited St. Margarets with my wife Mary, and what struck me most, was the bareness of the whole structure of the building. Nothing had really changed on close inspection, it had suffered no damage during the air raids, but I suppose a daytime visit, and being virtually empty just added to the feeling of almost unadorned bareness. My boyhood recollections were mainly of a church very full at services, with all the pomp which goes with high church worship, the choir wore black cassocks with a white surplice over, and a white frilled collar at the neck, the clergy, always two. Canon Duke-Baker, and father Copley were resplendent in the same garments as the choir except for the frilled collar, but with beautifully coloured, braided over capes etc. the correct names of these splendid garments I do not remember. One of the alter boys always carried an ornate brass container on chains in which was burnt incense, this he swung back, and forth as we came out of the vestry to proceed to the choir stalls for services. The precession of the servers, the choir, and the clergy must have been quite a site as it proceeded between the congregation towards the alter, I never saw it in all its glory, being privileged to be with the precession. My experience in the choir at this church set the pattern for my singing in a number of other churches as I moved around the county of Hampshire following my evacuation from Portsmouth, but more of that later.

When I look back over this period, it never ceases to amaze me how everyone managed to cope with the rigours of every day life, almost all things took twice as long to carry out, even the most menial of tasks such as shopping, not only because of the queuing, but the sheer difficulty of reaching ones destination, if say you had to cross to the other side of the city, quite often the trolley bus wires would be down or the electricity supply cut off closing down the transport system altogether, I think all mum's should have been awarded a medal for the way in which they overcame the almost insurmountable difficulties.

The continuing stress caused by the almost nightly air raids was beginning to tell on mother, the effort of surviving the daily routine taking their toll, and, following the night of the fire blitz she made a decision that was to alter our lives for ever.

The night of January 10th 1941 was chosen by the German Bomber Command to blitz Portsmouth with mainly incendiary bombs. All night waive after waive of enemy aircraft targeted the city, and it appeared to set fire to every building, not so of course, but that was how it appeared, I spent some of that night sitting in the shelter lobby watching this attempt at the mass destruction of my wonderful city, I will never forget that night, the whole city appeared to be glowing red, the morning arrived with a pall of black smoke hanging in the air. Many times in the years that followed we would see newsreels, when the cinemas were open, of cities like Portsmouth, and we would wonder how anyone ever survived, but those that did, carried on about their business as though nothing had happened, such was the courage of the normal Englishman, or should I be politically correct, and say English person.

Once the decision was made to evacuate the family, mum began the task of arranging the packing of the contents of our home to go into storage, and to say our goodbyes to all our friends, and family who would be staying behind, at least for a while. My two brothers, Ed, and Dennis went to a Naval home in Swanley, Kent, they may well have gone before the rest of us left for the country, but I cannot remember, they eventually joined Greenwich Naval School, and on completion of their time there, Ed joined the Navy as an Electrical Artificer, going on to be a Lt. Cdr. before retiring. Dennis followed in fathers footsteps, and joined the Royal Marine Band Service, when he retired he emigrated to Canada.

When finally we had packed our bags ready for the off, mum visited the neighbours,to say farewell, and I went to the butchers to see Arthur junior, and then on round to the church for my goodbyes to my dear friend father Copley, as you can imagine that was quite emotional, he had been such a comfort, not only to me, but to all the family, what I did not know at the time, was that was the last time I would see him. Some years after returning to the Portsmouth area I found out that he had taken up a post in the Isle of Wight, and had passed away there. We donned our outer clothing, slung our gas masks over our shoulder, and made our way to the point of departure, where that was I have no idea, probably the church or the school. One thing has always foxed me. where was my other brother Doug, and my sisters Daphne, and Sheila, I cannot recall them being with mother, but they must have been, because we finally ended up the same area of the countryside. Where we were going, we had no idea, all we knew was that we had a long journey by bus, and train to a destination in the country, as it turns out it was the tiny village of Faccombe, midway between Andover, and Newbury in the north of Hampshire, so in fact we did not travel too far, but it was another world. Our departure that day would be the end of an era for the whole family, not only were we going to somewhere quite unknown to us, but we were destined only to see one another on rare occasions for the rest of our lives.

Before moving on to a new chapter in my life, I would like to mention a few of my relatives who served with credit during the ensuing conflict. My mothers sister Hilda whose husband William served as a petty officer in the navy, his time being spent mainly in home waters, and the Middle East, survived the war, even though a cruiser in which he was serving was sunk. A brother of mums, Ron, was in the army, came through desert, and the European campaigns, he was a fine artist, and during the whole of his army career did pencil sketches of people he served with, officers, and all other ranks, all in caricature form. Dad's brother Albert, everyone knew him as Alb, was a chief petty officer in the Navy, one of the dreaded chief G.I's, he served in Singapore on motor torpedo boats, and when Singapore fell to the Japanese, the flotilla was scuttled, and thirty or so men, English, and Chinese including a wounded Chinese officer who had to be carried on a stretcher, walked through six hundred miles of enemy country to safety.

He survived the rest of the war. later becoming an instructor of merchant navy officers based on an old French man-o-war called Conway moored in the Menai Straits. North Wales. When I married, my wife, and I spent our honeymoon with him, and his dear wife Bertha. I must just mention that Alb had a son who quite recently tried to document his fathers exploits following his escape from Singapore, but despite his efforts, even at the highest level, the information is top secret, and will not be released until eighty years has elapsed from the time of the incident. What harm could possibly be done by putting this courageous episode into the public domain I cannot imagine, it would certainly make a wonderful film.

CHAPTER 7

The Village

The previous chapters, have I am aware, left gaping holes in the memory recall, only to be expected sixty odd years on, however, I know that from here on in things will improve because the following few years or so left such a lasting impression on me.

Travelling by train, and bus to my new home in Faccombe, was quite an ordeal, the train only ran as far as Andover, from there to Hurstbourne Tarrant was by bus, and normally a walk of sum three miles or so took you to the village, I cannot recall walking that last leg, so I imagine a special bus was laid on for us , some thirty odd children, and a few parents.

On finally arriving, we were assembled in the village hall, this incidentally was to become our school, we were lined up, rather reminiscent of a cattle market, and looked over by the female grownups who were to take us into there homes as paid boarders. What went through these village women's minds as they looked us over, I cannot think, but they made their choices, and away we went. A Mrs. Webb chose me, and a boy named Ken whose surname I cannot recall, an odd combination, because although he was the same age as myself, he was twice as big, and as it turns out, a bully, but like all bullies, proved to be a coward, and very lazy.

The house we were taken to was very modem, one of a pair, semi detached, and close to the outskirts of the village, constructed completely of cedar wood, was extremely warm in winter, and cool in the summer. Only one other feature stands out in my mind, that was the cooking stove, situated in the main living area, not the kitchen, I had no idea of the make at the time, but I can be almost sure now that it was an Agga, a little different from those seen these days, in fact it was set into a completely tiled surround, and consisted of four elements, a fire to one bottom corner with a front that dropped down to allow warming the room, and three enclosed ovens forming the square, the fire section had a space above to allow the boiling of a kettle, or heating pots.

The family of which we were to become part consisted of Mr.and Mrs. Webb, and their two son's, John the eldest, and Victor, who as it turns out was not to be around for too long, somehow he was called up into the army as a conscript, but John was allowed to continue as a farm labourer as an essential worker. Mr Webb senior, although getting on in years also worked on the farm. one thing I particularly remember about him was that after dinner in the evening he would always check his watches, two silver hunters on heavy chains, making sure that they were fully wound, and that the time was correct. He was a small man with a large bushy moustache, a wonderful man, of few words, but always willing to help if the need arose, I believe he passed away before his son Victor returned from the war, rather sad.

The village stood on a hill surrounded by rolling downs, and woods as far as the eye could see in every direction, and all owned by one family, in fact most of the village was also owned by them, the Hendersons. The approach was made along a valley which ran from Hurstboume Tarrant to Coombe. I must say that entering Hurstboume from the Andover road was quite hazardous, particularly in winter, that approach was very steep, and terminated at the bottom on a "T" junction in the village, it was quite a common occurrence for vehicles to crash into the cottages at the bottom, whilst I was there I remember hearing that a Bren Gun Carrier had careered down the hill out of control, ending up in the front room of one of the cottages on the other side of the "T" junction at the bottom, thankfully no one was injured.

Walking along the valley towards Coombe, a road branched off to the right, this led through a wooded area rising all the time until it flattened out for the approach to Faccombe. The first site of the village in those days were the grounds of the manor house to the right, the road went on past the gates to the house, and continued on through the village, where the road went to I cannot remember, I could consult a map, but that would not be true to my purpose. Two lanes led off to the left from the main through road, and met above the main farm area, the single lane continued on past what remained of the village until it connected with the valley at the bottom of the hill, at this junction was the hamlet of Netherton, a couple of houses, and a churchyard, no church, one of the houses was adjacent to the churchyard, and although I did not know it when I first arrived in Faccombe, I was eventually to live in that house.

In Faccombe itself there was a pub, a general store, and a church, very small as befits such a tiny community, if recollection serves me right it had an extremely tidy churchyard which in spring had a carpet of daffodils, there was also the village hall, what this was used for before us evacuees arrived I cannot imagine, because it did appear that the only social life was a visit to the pub, perhaps a pint of the best, and polite conversation was all that was necessary to suffice these, for the most part simple, uncomplicated, lovely people.

The main farm buildings, and yards, below which was the house where I was billeted, were very modern, and housed not only the cattle in winter, but had ample room to store feed, and all the machinery necessary to run such an estate, International Caterpillar tractors, a rubber tired Alice Chalmer tractor which had a gearbox similar to a car, this I remember because John later taught me to drive it, something which proved invaluable much later in my life when learning to drive a car. The farm also had several combined harvesters, this proved the wealth of the owners, as most farmers had to hire them, there was also a binder, seems odd when you take stock of all this modem equipment, but very necessary, as some of the hillsides were too steep for the combines to negotiate, quite often this binder was drawn by a pair of horses. Two Shires, and one Suffolk Punch were stabled at the farm, wonderful animals, many was the time I would ride the backs of one of these when on my way back from the fields with John at the end of his working day.

Below the house where I was living, on the hill towards Netherton was in impressive house called Pinewood, here lived the eldest son of the squire, with his family, a Capt. Pat Henderson, known locally as "Capt. Pat", he was in the army, and often away on duty, but always seemed to be around if there happened to be a social function, and always for a "shoot", my mother became his families cook/housekeeper.

The squire of the village was the Hon. Henderson, he, and his good lady lived in the large modern manor house on the approach road from Hurstbourne to Faccombe, just outside the village. No one saw much of Mrs. Henderson, but when the squire was not away on Parliamentary business we would see him everywhere taking an interest in everything that went on, so he should of course with such a vast estate under his sole ownership. One thing I can always remember him doing on a regular basis, was tending the grass verges around the boundary of the churchyard, they were kept immaculate, he would invariably be accompanied by his gun dogs, some eight or so black Retrievers, and one tan, and white Cocker Spaniel, generally recognised as the best dog of them all. They would run around him, and often annoy him, on one occasion I saw him heave a billhook at the pack of them, how he did not harm any of them I will never know.

The church had a resident priest. Canon Theophalas, I cannot be sure of the spelling, he seemed very old to us children, perhaps because of his white hair, more likely, to all children of our age, grown- ups over about the age of twenty years or so always appeared old!! The church had no choir, so one of the first priorities after our arrival was to form one under the auspices of the lady organist. I cannot remember having choir practice, but I imagine we must have done, unless we just sang what was put in front of us, to the villagers anything must have been better than none at all, I certainly enjoyed being part of a choir again. On certain occasions when the choir was not required, I would take a turn at pumping the organ bellows, a simple, and effective way of ensuring the organ had plenty of air.

The farm itself, because of the restrictions existing throughout the war, was mostly arable, that is fields of wheat, barley, oats, with some potatoes, other items such as kale, sugar beet etc. were grown for cattle feed to supplement the shortfall in the amount of hay produced. One herd of cows produced milk for the whole village, what a herd this was, fine Redpoles, a breed with no horns, and an all over colour of red/brown, one very large bull serviced this herd at the appropriate time, otherwise he rarely saw the light of day, he was though pampered the whole time as befit's a pedigree animal of his stature. The herd warranted a cowman, and it was while I was living in Faccombe that he was called up for the armed forces, he must of wanted to go, because as an essential worker he could have stayed put, however his replacement wanted accommodation close to the *farm*, the Webb's house was the most suitable, and being "tied" we were moved to Netherton, looking back, the method of employment was feudal to say the least, and would probably not have been tolerated in this day, and age.

A very important employee was the gamekeeper, as I understand, not strictly legal during the war years, because the need of humans over birds was given priority, however, a great many very important personages lived around the area at this time, so game birds were bred, on that I will enlarge later.

Faccombe boasted a pond, not large, but very attractive with high banks to one side, and full of wildlife, insects of every description, frogs, dragonflies etc. When in winter it froze over it formed a perfect ice rink, no skating, but plenty of sliding, we would hurtle down the bank, and slide across to the opposite side, many a tumble occurred, but never any serious injuries.

Reading this you will have gathered that I am painting a picture of a idyllic pastoral village, that is exactly what it was, the inhabitants knew nothing of the war except that which they read in the papers, or heard on the radio, no television in those days, and of course should any of them had family in armed forces, other information, limited though it would have been, filtered through as well. The odd aircraft would occasionally be seen in the sky, because there were air bases reasonably close, but to all intent, and purpose, no physical sign of war was apparent, this then was the environment in which I was to live for the next eighteen months or so.

CHAPTER 8

A New Inception

Somehow I had imagined that the tranformation from city boy to country lad would have been difficult, my only country experience previously was the annual Sunday school outing for a day, with games of rounders, followed by a picnic tea, in fact it was not at all difficult, and the trauma of losing my dad gradually began to fade.

Living in the Webb household, was, at first, hard to come to terms with, not so much the house itself, I had a comfortable bed, it was warm, no easy chairs to sit in, but what lad worries about that, and Mrs Webb's kindness itself, no, it was the food. The day would begin with porridge, and toast, except in the summer months when, whatever cereal was available would be served, I hated porridge. Lunch would consist of meat of some sort, and although beef, lamb, pork, and the like were in short supply, we would often have rabbit, hare, pidgeon, and even pheasant when in season, fresh vegetables from the garden, and always boiled potatoes, very rarely gravy. At that time I disliked most vegetables, and did not care much for boiled potatoes, at least when they were not mashed, and I have always liked a vehicle to help the meal down. Tea was usually boiled eggs, bread, and jam, toast, cake, and the like, that was okay, the eggs were always fresh, the jam, and cake homemade, it was really the monotony of the potatoes, and the vegetables that used to get to me. Looking back I suppose I was rather ungrateful, I certainly lived a much better life than I would have done had I still lived in Portsmouth.There was little shortage of most essential foods, fresh milk could be purchased daily at the dairy, and eggs from the farm, I would go, and collect them from the hen houses in the field adjacent to the farm, butter although not plentiful was sometimes also available at the farm. All vegetables, potatoes, and fruit were grown in the Webb's garden, so you see we were almost self sufficient. Meat was the commodity most in short supply, and only the amount indicated on the ration books would be supplied by the butcher from Hurstboume Tarrant, she, I remember it being a lady, would do the rounds of the villages on a Saturday in her small van, if you were lucky sometimes you would be able to buy a little offal. Other household goods not available in the village shop would be supplied by a mobile shop making occasional visits to the surrounding villages, and sometimes from making a visit to Andover, if there was a need to buy such things as clothes.

The house I have described, it was close to the road, but at a lower level, a quite steep short curving path ran directly from the road to the front door. At the top of the path was a row of trees which the locals called "bush", they had dark bark, long thorns, and small leaves not unlike oak, maybe Hawthorne? These were in great demand as firewood because they had the quality of being slow burning, adjacent to the hedge of trees was a shed where all the garden tools were kept, together with the sawhorse, cross-cut saws of every type, and axes to split the logs, these were of differing weights, and the one I was to learn to use, was one of five pounds.

The gardens to the front, and rear of the property were large, enabling John, and his father to grow all the needs of the household, I remember one thing that fascinated me as a boy, was the way marrows were grown. Firstly a mound of horse manure would be placed in an appropriate part of the garden, something like five feet by five feet, and one foot in height, a thin layer of sifted earth would be spread on the top, and the seeds planted, as soon as these started to grow a layer of fresh straw was laid over the top, and sides, it would be no exaggeration to say that the resultant marrows were huge, I did not however show much interest in them, to me it was just another vegetable to dislike. Years later I did taste them baked in the oven, I cannot say that the dislike persisted, I had in those early days only tried them boiled, and they always seemed to be wet, soggy, and with very little taste.

As a boy from the city, it was the sights, sounds, and smells of the countryside that were to leave me with an abiding love of nature that would stay with me for the rest of my life. One of my earliest recollections of sight, and smell, was from a copse not too far from the house, it always seemed to smell of onions, but I am sure it was wild garlic, and being spring when I arrived, the whole area was covered in bluebells. Most of the woods on the estate had an abundance of wild flowers including daffodils, and the banks everywhere were carpeted with small wild flowers. Over the years the wild flowers throughout England all but disappeared, mainly due to pollution of one sort or another, but today there is a great awareness of the need to preserve the natural habitat, and the planting of seeds forms part of the contract when building new motorways etc., long may it continue.

School as I said previously took part in what was the village hall, all the children, a little over thirty of us were all taught in the one area, segregated according to age, and taught by two elderly ladies, neither of these I knew, but I suppose most have come from schools in Portsmouth. All subjects previously taught to us were covered, mainly maths, English, and general knowledge, with nature study thrown in for good measure, this often took the form of field trips when we would collect wild flowers for pressing, and mounting in scrap books, this would be rather frowned upon today, but in those days was the perfect way to be taught about the wonders of nature. School work, although undertaken with some enthusiasm came rather low on the priority list, there was so much more to do once we had completed our daily studies, when the bell sounded, we could not wait to get away, much like today. I must tell you of an incident that happened on my way to school one day, I was walking across this field, and because I was early, climbed a tree, as I often did, and was sitting in a forked branch at the end of a bow watching the rabbits, they were around in great numbers in those days before mixamatosis killed off most of the population. I must have been some eight to ten feet from the ground, and completely pre-occupied with my thoughts when I heard the school bell, I dropped to the ground, my knees came up to meet my face, and my two front teeth buried themselves in one of my knees, they made a fair cut, and that scar is still to be seen to this day.

Life in the country suited me very well, I did not see much of mother, but at the time it did not seem to matter, children are great survivors, often almost alone, I was lucky in that I saw more of her than most of the children, in fact I do not recall any other children with parents residing in or near to the village. During my time here I saw my brothers Ed, and Den only once, I travelled to Swanley in Kent with mother, presumably by bus, and train, and must have stopped overnight, but I certainly cannot remember, where they lived, at Naval School, they were subjected to a harsh regime, much as normal recruits joining the Royal Navy would have been, I would certainly have not liked the discipline, does no one any harm of course, but having someone shouting at you the whole time, ones freedom being curtailed by communal living, queuing for all meals etc., not for me, strangely enough, not too long in the distant future, I was to experience part of that way of life, and have to admit that I quite enjoyed certain elements of it.

The seasons in the country are not only dictated by the weather, but also by the requirements of the farm, and this in turn by the demands of the Agricultural Ministry during time of war, on the surface nothing appeared to change, one assumes there were changes, but I suspect that because of the position of the local squire, all went much as it had always done.

I enjoyed all facets of the seasons as they occurred, everything was new, and I really wanted to learn as much as I could about the growing of crops, harvesting, habitat, and the wildlife, to this end I was to indulge myself to the full.

CHAPTER 9

Spring

Arriving in late spring, I missed most of the land preparation, and planting, but not all, as the seasons follow for the most part a set pattern, I can mirror the following spring. The winters were very harsh in the north of Hampshire, difficult to believe when you think, I was only about fifty miles north of my home city, so occasionally the ploughing was delayed by this inclement weather.

As I said, most of the preparation of the soil was complete by the time of my arrival in Faccombe, but because the farmhands often had to work long hours to complete the required tasks, I would often join John out in the fields after school, we had no homework in those days, so leisure time it was. For me it was a time to improve my ever growing knowledge of life on the farm, and John, very much the father figure, was only too pleased to impart his considerable experience of the land to me.

You may think from what I have said that it was all physical work out of school, time, but that was not so, I liked to walk in the woods, and because every farmhand had a stick, John helped me find a suitable straight length of Hazel with branches growing from a knot at the top to make my own stick for walking. He roughly cut the branch away from the root, and trimmed the top branches off, I finished it, cleaning the bottom, and cutting the top to leave a clean knot ball, ideal for dealing with rabbits. Everyone carried a penknife, and I soon acquired one, essential to fashion a walking stick from rough timber. I would hesitate to call mine a "walking stick" because it was used for a number of things, from cutting the undergrowth away when walking the woods, to clubbing rabbits on the run, when you are young, and fit you can outrun a rabbit, but not a hare, they are much too fast, I would just add, that you would have very little chance of catching a rabbit if it was seen in a wood, because it would run in all directions in, and, out of the trees, but in an open field you would stand every chance of catching the following days dinner.

That spring taught me about the planting of corn, i.e. wheat, barley, and oats by means of a distributor, this was a machine approximately twelve feet wide, and mounted on two steel wheels, it consisted basically of a metal container with holes in the bottom above which was a rotating worm, turned by being connected to the wheels, the container had a series of lids to the top allowing access for filling with the grain seed. This simple piece of machinery was towed back, an forth across the field by tractor, the wheels would show the area which had already been sown, the turning worm within the container would ensure even distribution of the seed, when this part of the process was complete the field would be rolled. The rollers used on this farm consisted of three separate rollers of cast iron, ribbed along their length, each about six feet long, and two feet in diameter, these were fixed to an iron frame in a staggered position to ensure that the complete area covered was rolled.

I would just watch, and inwardly digest everything that was going on, sometimes I would be allowed to stand alongside John on the tractor, but that was more than a little dangerous, so we had to ensure that the foreman was nowhere to be seen for fear of John getting into trouble.

During that late spring I had my first taste of working in the nursery, at the time it seemed like a nursery, but was in fact the gardens attached to the manor house. Every requirement for the house kitchen was grown here, together with all the desert fruits that would be required for the house itself, and, last but by no means least, flowers of every description. My task was nothing too demanding, washing clay pots, and there were hundreds of them. The potting shed had a large galvanised tub full of warm water, heated by an electrical element, around the walls were differing width shelves, all I had to do was scrub the pots with a brush, and when clean, stack them on the shelves to dry ready for planting out the various seedlings. The job itself was boring, but it enabled me to be looked upon as trustworthy for any future work that may become available, and of course earn a few shillings.

We had settled into a routine at school with all the pupils working to the best of their ability, the war having deprived them of regular tuition until this time. Field trips became more frequent as the weather improved, there was much to see, and hear, some of the children collected wild bird egg's, piecing each end with a pin, and blowing in one end to remove the yolk, and white, gathering these egg's was a good way to identify the birds, but looking back was all very cruel, and would be considered criminal today. Looking for rabbits became a major past time, and, because my only weapon was a stick, I decided to make myself a bow of yew, now it was always said that the finest bow's in England were made from yew, but found great difficulty in finding a branch straight enough from which to fashion one, I eventually found one near enough straight, and made my bow from that. Arrows were quite another thing, they were made from hazel, which was plentiful here about, and wonderfully straight, I made many, pointing one end, and cutting slots at the other to take the flight feathers. Now although this bow was not overly straight, it outfired anything the other children made, but it did not make me very successful at shooting rabbits, or for that matter anything else, but it was great fun to use.

As spring turned to summer, the whole school was looking forward to the long summer holiday, most of them would be going home or to relatives living in safe areas, but not myself, my mother lived close by, so I was able to look forward to six weeks of free time around the farm, taking in another set of experiences, as yet unknown to me. Why is it that summers past always seem so much better than they are today, nobody appears to be able to answer that question, and yet most agree with it, I was to enjoy this time of year, probably as much as anything I would experience in the future.

Before going on to that first summer, I must tell you of a crop grown here about in quite large quantities. Flax, something not usually associated with England, but very important during the years of the war. Flax is one of those plants where the roots, stem, and seed heads all have a use, my memory does not serve me too well on the use of the seeds, but I believe drug companies used the roots, and the stems were used to make cloth, and rope. The machine employed to harvest this plant looked rather like a binder in that it had a large paddle at the front which pushed the stems into a fork in turn lifting the plant from the ground on to a travelling bed, this conveyed it to the main body of the machine where it was bundled, tied around with string, and thrown out of the side. The bundles would then have to be collected by hand, stacked into what was known as a "stook" to dry out, and in such a manner as to allow the air to pass through for more rapid drying.

CHAPTER 10

Summer

That first summer opened my eyes to so many new, and wonderful things, the bird calls, and songs, the sight, and colour of different trees, the fields with their swaying corn, wheat with neat seed pods pointing towards the sky, barley, much shorter seed pods rather like wheat, but with course spikes from each seed, and of course, oats, much taller with seed pods hanging in bunches like flowers. Other fields were planted with sugar beet, this was processed for the home market, large white cabbages, and kale, these grown for animal feed during the winter months. The white cabbage often "found" its way on to the tables of the farm hands, and I would often harvest mushrooms from under the kale in the early morning when the dew was at its heaviest, I always ended up very wet from the waist down, but the mushrooms were magnificent.

Some additional help for the harvest came from what I thought an unusual source, "land girls", teenage girls, and women drafted into an army of workers specifically to help on the land. They wore fawn jodhpurs, long green socks, heavy brown shoes, fawn shirt, green jumper, and rimmed hat. They were expected to work as hard as the normal farm hands, many of them found this difficult, quite apart from their natural strength they were for the most part from the cities, and not used to this type of physical work. One of the girls I befriended, not because she was of the female species, I was much too young to appreciate her "attributes", no, she had a bicycle, not her own, but one she hired from a lady in the village, it was one of those known as a "sit up and beg", a large ladies bike with a curved down tube, and complete with a rack over the rear mudguard, this had a series of strings to each side which terminated at the wheel hub, these were supposed to stop the ladies skirts getting caught in the wheel, quite a good idea except when the need arose to clean the bike, then you cursed them. I am sure I rode that bike more than she did, I could not reach the saddle, but I thought it was great. I did not know it at the time, but this was the beginning of a hobby which would mature into a very serious sport for me until I was drafted for National Service in 1951, and since has been of continuing interest, in particular following continental road racing on television.

You will remember my saying that Faccombe had a pond, this teemed with all manner of life except fish, early in the year one of our interests as children was collecting frog spawn, and keeping them in jam jars until newts hatched out finally having to return them to the pond from whence they came. Now with the approach of summer the pond became a cacophony of sound, more discordant than disagreeable. Here I saw my first dragonfly, this very beautiful insect, with, in this case, a bright blue body, and a wing span of some five inches or more, moving at an incredible speed, then hover, then shoot off, and hover again at another part of the pond. It is difficult to imagine that this creature had lain dormant under the water for so long, and when it finally immerges into the sunlight only lives for a few hours, ours is not to reason why, only to wonder at this phenomena of nature.

The periphery of the pond was a haven for us children at play, it had trees, bushes, long grass, rushes etc. together with the sights, and sounds of many birds, frogs, and grasshoppers, most used it as a play area, but I, being the loner that I was even in those days would sit, and watch, and on some occasions I would try, and draw what I was watching. I was taking a keen interest in sketching, and when I moved on in my school career became quite proficient, but drawing mainly landscapes, and still life, I was never very good at animals or humans.

There was great activity in late spring, and early summer with hay making, now a more essential task in wartime than peace, because the cattle have to be fed well during the winter whatever may be going on around, yield was all important. The machine for cutting the grass was basically a series of knives crossing one another at almost ground level with a small platform at the rear to guide the grass over, and on to the ground behind, this structure was about six feet wide, and was towed by a tractor. Once the field was cut, the grass was turned by means of a mechanical rake, well, a series of rakes, forming long mounds winding back, and forth across the field allowing for ease of drying. The cut grass was regularly inspected, and as needed, the whole process of turning was repeated until it was dry. Now, on most farms the dried hay would be carted to somewhere close to the farm, and built into a rick, a solid structure resembling a house complete with a pitched roof, and even thatching to keep out the inclement weather, during the winter this would be dismembered for feeding the cattle.

This estate though had a very different method of storage. In the actual farmyard itself were several corrugated iron structures, probably about twenty feet in diameter which could be made as high as was practical for removal of the contents later, these were called silo's. I have since that time, seen these complete with a roof, but as I recall, those in Faccombe had tarpaulins to keep out the rain. The hay was layered from the ground level up with-alternate layers of black treacle, and as the days went by more layers were added to take up the settling, whatever process went on between the hay, and the treacle, I do not know, but one thing was certain, a very rich feed was produced for the lucky cattle. The black treacle had another good use in those far off austere days, as Mr Kipling would say, "it makes exceedingly good cakes", need I say more!!

As the weather began to improve, and get warmer, the corn began to ripen, and as always, the hope was that the harvesting would take place during July, the dread was always the possibility of storms, with the rain flattening the crop, and preventing the ripening process. Had this happened, the farmhands would be sent out to the fields with pitch forks to lift the crop clear of the ground, often this lifting had little effect, and when ready for harvest, the affected area's often had to be cropped by hand with a scythe.

The wealth of the squire was very apparent when the machinery for harvesting was brought out from the barns where they had been stored for the winter, three combine harvesters, and a baler. Most farmers hired this equipment, the capital outlay was too much for all except those with very healthy bank balances. Today all combines are self propelled, but when I was a boy they were quite rare, this farm had only one, the others were hauled by large International caterpillar tractors. Combines are so named because their function was to cut the crop, remove the seed heads, and despatch the straw through a shute at the rear. On the opposite side to the cutters on those being towed, was a shute from which came the husked seed, a man stood here on a platform with a sack, when the sack was full he would shut off the flow of seed, tie off the sack with binder string, throw the sack onto the ground, and commence the process again. The self propelled combine had the rotors, and cutters in the front, and was driven from a cab mounted high above these cutters, giving a wonderful view, and a great sense of power, it was quite a site to see these combines, each cutting some twelve feet of crop at a time, starting at the outside of the field, and traversing the perimeter of the crop until all is harvested.

Depending on the availability of labour, on some occasions the baler would follow the combines, collecting the straw. Most people are aware of the normal size of a bale, but have you ever wondered how the bale is so tightly bound with wire? The baler would collect the straw from the ground at the front, and it would be conveyed into a square shute the bale size, and compressed with a ram, it then continues into a partly open shute on either side of which sit one or two men holding baling wire of a determined length, the ram would then compress the straw into half the normal length, the men would quickly thread the wire through the appropriate section, and wind the ends together before the ram was released, and sprung the bale back to the normal size. The finished bale would continue along the open section at the rear, and dropped to the ground ready to be collected by flat back truck, and transported to a barn for storage. I have said that men operated the wire tying operation, but on a number of occasions I too sat there, and helped out, I believe it was a case of young nimble fingers being applied to a job normally requiring more strength.

When the combines had finished their work, the sacks of seed would be collected on a flat back trailer, and taken to the dryer. What was interesting about this part of the operation was that often the Shire horses were brought out, I would get very excited then, because I knew that in all probability I would be allowed to ride one of them back to the stable at the end of the day, remove the harness, and feed him. I say "him" because all three of the horses kept were stallions.

The dryer mentioned previously was situated at the bottom of the hill connecting Faccombe with Netherton, and close to the road running through the valley. This resembled a large barn constructed of corrugated iron sheets, and having a pitched roof, but no windows. Inside, a number of machines were interconnected so that the seed would travel from one section to the other somewhat like a production line. The threshed seed would be tipped onto a flat bed of perforated metal mounted above the floor, this vibrated allowing all the remaining husks to be shaken off, I believe this bed had hot air pumped through the underside.The seed would, after this part of the process was complete be carried through the building by means of small buckets attached to conveyer belts, tipping the seed into the next part of the operation, and so on until the cycle was complete, when once again the dried seed would be bagged up, and transported to a local mill for converting to flour or whatever. The building was almost too hot for comfort, but necessary to ensure that the seed dried perfectly, this was the final piece of the jigsaw which allowed the corn to be cut, and turned into flour in one day, a highly profitable operation, and good for the economy of the country.

I must tell you of one of the jobs within the dryer that had to be completed before the summer, that was the cleaning of the first stage, the perforated bed. As you can appreciate, many of the holes, and there were thousands of them, would get blocked transporting the grain from one end to the other, so the holes would have to be punched clear through with a brad hole, a labour intensive job, on your hands, and knees, and one that would test your patience to the limit.

The time of harvest was great for those of us who loved being out in the fields where all the action was taking place. We would follow the combines a few yards back from the cutters, treading the stubble which was usually about six inches in height, I of course with my trusty stick at the ready. Rabbits seem to have a six sense where the blades of the combine were concerned, they would crouch down low enough to allow the cutters to pass over them, only to be faced by the lads chasing them all over the field screaming like banchees. One of the rabbits main line of defence was to run in ever changing directions making it extremely difficult to keep up with them let alone noble them, but, on quite a number of occasions I would triumph, and rabbit pie would be on the menu the following day.

I remember on one occasion I caught a young hare, a leveret, and the land girl who used to lend me her bike wanted to look at it before I killed it, a meal for the cat. I duly let her look at it, then held it by the back legs, took hold of its neck, pulled, and twisted the way John had shown me to do, it not only killed the defenceless creature, but its head came off, the land girl screamed, and ran off, I cannot remember whether she ever lent me her bike again!! Another method of killing rabbits was to hold them by the back legs, and give them a sharp blow to the back of the neck with the edge of your hand, I did not have the strength to do that, but it was common practice by the farm hands, such was the way of life in the countryside at that time.

Another practice common here abouts, was trapping rabbits, and two methods were employed, snares, and gin traps, both outlawed now of course on humanitarian grounds, I was not allowed to lay gin traps, I rather doubt that I could have sprung them in any case, but I used to accompany John when he would set perhaps six or more along the rabbit runs, easily seen in the hedgerows, and woods, I would set snares on similar runs. The snares I would make myself with a stake, and a looped wire attached, the stake was driven into the ground at the side of the run, and the loop set upright across the run hidden as much as possible by the grass. The poor unsuspecting rabbit would tear along his run, catch his neck in the wire loop, it would tighten, and strangle it, one point I would make, these traps were set in the evening, and inspected the following morning, should any animal still be alive, it was quickly put out of its misery. Looking back on this practice, it all appeared rather barbaric, but it was the way things were, country folk thought it natural to hunt food in this way, and how could you argue when meat was in short supply, even if very little else was.

Although I had only lived in the country for a short while, I was beginning to talk in the vernacular, the north Hampshire dialect is broad, rather like the tongue you would encounter in Cornwall, although I doubt that any Cornish person would agree with me. I did not find this a problem until I eventually moved to another school in the south of Hampshire where the dialect is much different, I was then saddled with the title of "yokel" this I was only able to discard after about a year of study at a somewhat higher level.

You may wonder how as children we were able to have so much time to pursue our out of school activities, well, the summer evening were much longer in those days, the introduction of double summer time during those war years enabled the likes of farmers to work often until ten o'clock at night, very necessary because sometimes it was not possible to commence harvesting until mid morning due to the extremely heavy dew, the fields earmarked to be worked would be inspected at regular intervals from dawn until the word was given to commence, once the foreman gave the word, all was a hive of activity.

The summer was drawing to an end, the days shortening, and the air getting cooler, time for fresh pursuits, and more experiences to be stored in the memory. School now became the most time consuming element in my life, and not only because the evenings were drawing in, as they say, but I was informed that the following spring I would be sitting the grammar school exam, not by my mother, but by one of the teachers, no consultation with me on this most important of matters, perhaps that is what was done in those days, I do not know, however, it meant that for the first time in my life I would have to take my studies a great deal more seriously to enable me, hopefully, to pass. I remember that teacher telling me "that was what my father would have wanted", something I could not very well argue with.

A couple of memorable things happened at the tail end of that summer, one because of the fear I felt at the time, and the other because I now know that I witnessed something rarely seen.

I had this particular day taken a walk along the valley towards Hurstbourne, but before reaching the village, turned left up the hill through the woods towards Faccombe, you will remember that at the approach to the village, on the right, was the manor house, a quite steep bank from the edge of the road led up to the boundary of the extensive gardens, and, at one point fruit trees over-hung the bank, among them apples. These proved too much of a temptation to me, remember I had walked some way, and was in need of sustenance! I climbed the bank, "scrumped" an apple, and walked on home enjoying my feast. Little did I know, but I had been seen, who by, I never found out, all I do remember is that I was summoned from school the following morning to report to the manor house.

I had no idea what I was going there for, but all was to become clear when I was ushered into the vast drawing room, and there standing in front of the fireplace was Lady Henderson, and a police constable, apparently he had travelled from his base in Hurstbourne on his bicycle, and looked none too pleased about it. I was given a stem lecture, first by the lady of the house on the wrong I had done, and then by the constable on the probable outcome of my offence should it ever happen again. I stood there absolutely terrified, I must have thought at the time that I had committed a major crime, finally I was allowed to go back to school, and eventually I was able to forget the matter, strangely, Lady Henderson never held this incident against me, later I was often allowed to work in the gardens of the house, and on a number of occasions, pass the time of day with her, I do believe that a point was made to all the evacuees at my expense.

The second memory concerned an incident of nature at it's most savage, again I was out walking, and had entered a field because a rabbit attracted my attention, it appeared to be sitting up quite still as though it was mesmerised, as it turns out it was, I had not noticed, out to my left there was a disturbance in the grass, all of a sudden this small creature like a squirrel, with a tan upper body, white underside, and black tip to it's tail, darted across the small section of open ground to where the rabbit sat, leapt on to it's back, and bit into the neck, there was an initial screech, and the rabbit was dead. The deed was no sooner done, and the animal ran off with the prey, perhaps it had a family to feed, I was never to know. When I arrived home that evening I recalled the incident to John, and he told me the animal was a stoat, I had no idea at the time just how rare that sighting was, and it was not until quite recently while watching a programme on television devoted entirely to the habits of this beautiful creature that I knew just how privileged I had been.

CHAPTER 11

Autumn

With the onset of autumn, I had wondered how I was to occupy my time after school, however, I need not have worried, and many new experiences were to come my way thanks to John.

Towards the end of the summer holidays, an opportunity arose to earn some pocket money. One quite large field was given over to growing potatoes, this I believe was a requirement of the Ministry of Agriculture because it was impossible to import from the Continent, and, when it was time to lift the crop, every available hand was mustered including the evacuees to hand lift the potatoes. The machine for getting them out of the ground was basically a rotating circular rake, horse drawn because they could walk between the heaped rows, and do very little damage.

We were all given a galvanised bucket to collect the potatoes in, and when this was full, or in the case of us children, when there was as much as we could carry, we had to take them to the edge of the field where they would be stacked. First a layer of straw was put on the ground, and the potatoes would be piled into a triangular form, approx. 4'0" at the base, and 4' 0" in height, as you can imagine by the time the crop was lifted the stack was very long, the whole was covered in a thick layer of straw, and then earth, every few feet along the apex the straw was allowed to pertrude through the earth to allow breathing, and cooling.

Potato lifting was extremely hard work, even for the grownups, however, for us children there was one great incentive, money, 12 shillings, and 6 pence for the week to be precise, a fortune in those days, and well worth the back ache.

Throughout the autumn, and winter, presumably to satisfy the needs of the village, and the local shops, the stack would be uncovered, sorted, and put into sacks. This was a thankless task, mucky, and smelly because quite a number of the potatoes would have started to rot, and to add to all this the ground was often covered in snow, one can only assume that the effort was worth while,

I am going to digress for a moment now, quite recently whilst on a trip to the country, a stop at a pub brought to mind another memory of something we were learning to do at school. In the car park, Morris dancers were performing, no, we were not taught Morris dancing, but country dancing, a similar thing you might say, and you would be partly right, the big difference was that we did not dress up in colourful costumes complete with bells. Country dancing is carried out in formation by boys, and girls, all the differing dances having their own steps, and movements, and there are many of them, taking quite a time to perfect, I can only recall one, and that was "Roger de Covelly", probably spelt incorrectly, but I am sure those more knowledgeable reading this will forgive me.

Back to the text, I had noticed that during the preceeding few months many more pheasants, and partridges were on the wing, these had been bred in the woods, and were now almost ready for the shooting season due to commence in October. There would be regular "shoots" according to John, and he told me that I would be able to join the beaters for the day, and get paid for it. I would have gone along, and helped out for nothing, being paid for doing something I considered such fun was a bonus not to be missed.

School progressed much as usual except with xmas on the horizon preparations were under way for entertainment within the school, and for the Nativity play which was to be performed in the church. I cannot recall being in the nativity play probably because of my commitment to the choir, but I can remember that I made a puppet theatre with all the characters, these were moved about the stage by hand to the dialogue, written, and spoken by yours truly. I was not the only member of the school to make these miniature theatres, but I am sure that on the day of the actual performance just before breaking up for the Christmas holidays, mine received the greatest ovation, what do you mean, big head!! The Nativity play was something unique to this very small community, there not in normal circumstances being enough children in the village to perform this much loved act to commemorate the birth of Jesus. This one act play written by the teachers went down very well with all the local dignitaries as well as the villagers who normally attended church, the village in many ways was in a time warp, quite a number of the villagers felt they had to attend if the lord, and lady of the manor were sitting in their pew at the front of the church, however on this occasion I believe it was curiosity that brought most of them to church on that day.

I digress, I must go back to the end of the summer, the harvest had been gathered, most of the stubble had been burnt down to the earth, and ploughing the fields ready for planting of early crops was underway, crops being rotated field to field much as it had been done for hundreds of years. Vegetables such as turnips, white cabbage, and kale are lifted, and stored for use as cattle feed during the winter months when they have to be kept inside. The winters in this part of Hampshire can be quite severe, and although the cattle can withstand the cold, they would not be able to reach the pasture for feed.

Most of what I was to learn during the next few months would stand me in good stead much later in my life, although I was not aware of this at the time. It was not so much that I would necessarily use the actual skills, but that they taught me things like care, and attention to detail.

As previously said, October was the start of the pheasant, and partridge shooting season, and dates were drawn up for shoots every few weeks. The estate around Faccombe was vast, very many acres of rich woodland, almost unknown to me at this time, that would all change as time went on, until I knew the paths like the back of my hand. The farm hands, and certain of us older boys were not allowed to shoot of course, but would act as beaters, driving the birds towards the guns.

I looked forward to the first shoot with some trepidation, mainly I think, because I was afraid I would make some ghastly mistake, I need not have worried, John gave me all the pointers to allow me to enjoy my first day with the beaters.

The starting point for each shoot, and they differed for each session during the day, was determined by the game keeper, he would instruct us as to where to start, and we would all fan out, and await the signal to commence our treck. Sometimes this entailed walking across open country, sometimes through the woods, but more often than not, included both.

Once we heard the gamekeepers whistle blast, we would all start walking, we all carried sticks to allow us to beat down the undergrowth during our passage through the wooded areas, sometimes we would encounter quite difficult terrain, and progress would be slow, but eventually we arrived at the point where we had to stop to avoid being shot at, bare in mind that the birds were being driven straight into the path of the awaiting guns.

As we approached the guns, the noise was quite deafening, each member of the party had a pair if twelve bore shotguns, one being loaded while the other was being shot, usually there were at least twelve guns so you can imagine the noise when they were discharged. The birds, having been shot or flown over the heads of the guns, the signal would be given, and we would move on to the next location.

Previously I mentioned the Hon. Henderson's dog's, these would be out in force the days of the shoot to retrieve the fallen birds, these were loaded into a land rover to be transported back to the farm at the end of the day, it was not uncommon to have a "bag" in excess of three hundred birds after any one shoot, everyone was happy, and I imagine it must have been very profitable. A lunch break was always observed, and if we were close enough to the farm we would all assemble in a barn, sit on straw bales, and eat fresh bread, and cheese washed down with beer for the men, and ginger beer in stone bottles for us boy's, great fun. After this break, we would all set off again for the start of the next trek, this would go on until the light began to fade, and the gamekeeper called a halt.

I would be totally exhausted at the end of the day, and often my legs would be covered in scratches because I only wore short trousers, and boots in those days, in fact it was to be some two or three years before I eventually had my first pair of long trousers, and had to suffer quite a lot of abuse over that in the intervening time.

I must tell you a little about the guns, I can remember that there were only gentlemen, mostly dressed in plus- four suits, and deer stalker hats, very few were recognised except the Hon Henderson, his son Capt "Pat", and, if he was home from school, his younger brother who was about fourteen years old, and he was the only boy to carry a gun, a smaller bore shot-gun called a 4/10, I used to feel quite envious of him, often wondering what it would be like to be holding that gun.

Previous to one shoot, a great buzz went around the village because it was put about that some very important personages would attend, no names of course, and those of us among the beaters had to wait until the end of the first trek of the day to identify who they were. When we had completed that first phase, I was still none the wiser as to who the two gentlemen were. One was tall, and elegant, not dressed for shooting, he wore a long dark overcoat, and a homburg hat, the other was shorter, and rather rotund, obviously a lot younger, but already losing his hair, he was dressed in complete shooting garb.

I was curious to know who these two men were, and John informed me that the older of them was King Haaken of Norway, and the younger man was his son Prince Olaf, it would appear that they both lived in exile somewhere near to Newbury. Norway was fiercely pro British, but had been overrun by the German army. When the war finally came to an end, they returned to their own country to once more take up their rightful place as heads of the monarchy. They both in turn reigned their country, until their death, Norway still has a monarchy, and Harold is now king. Both of these gentlemen were to be seen on future shoots, and gives some intimation of the circle that the Henderson family moved in.

Following my first ever trek, I was curious to see what had been shot, and was surprised to see among the pheasants, partridges, and the odd hare, and rabbits, that most beautiful of birds, the Jay. Apparently, despite the restrictions imposed during the war, the hat making industry still flourished, and the feathers of this bird were much in demand. I rather think that it took a good eye to spot one of these, and to hit it at a distance that did not destroy the bird completely.

You will remember my saying that the cooking stove burnt either coal or wood, and a great deal was required to keep it going throughout the winter months, and, to this end the Hon. Henderson allowed each family a cart load of logs. Often new paths were being cut through the woods, and the trunks of the trees would be left at the side of the tracks. On a Saturday when John was not required to work, he would walk up to the farm yard, collect the rubber tyred Alice Chalmer tractor, hitch up a flat bottom trailer, and we would go into the woods to collect the lumber. That trailer was loaded to its limits, and took us quite a few hours before we could make our way back home, and unload, over the next few months this was cut into logs either by John or myself, and split into small logs with an axe, I would use the smaller five pound axe, any kindling required would be split from the logs with a bill hook, a sharp bladed tool which was short, wide, and with a curved head much like the beak of a bird, this was also used to lop braches from trees.

On one of these trips out with John, we had stopped to take a drink from the flask of tea that he always carried in what I imagined was on old army gas mask bag with a shoulder strap, it seemed a standard piece of equipment for all the farmhands to carry, after he had drunk his tea he pulled from his pocket a small tin box, emptied a small amount of brown dust on to the back of his hand, and promptly sniffed it up his nose, it was snuff, I had never seen it before, and after being offered it to try, did so, only to find that I had a lasting sneezing fit!

The days were now getting shorter, more, and more the farmhands were being found work within the confines of the farm buildings, clearing out the cowsheds where layer upon layer of straw, and dung had piled up, sometimes a foot thick, this was loaded onto flat bed trucks, and transported to the fields where it would be spread ready for ploughing into the ground. Cleaning the horse gear, another job which would normally have been low on the priority scale, the horses here, although magnificent creatures, were kept only for working with, and were never shown in the manner in which we see them today.

School concentrated more on the approaching festivities than the academic side of things, in fact I can only think of one thing that gave any indication of the approach to Christmas in the Webb household, and that was the making of Christmas puddings. These were made in the traditional way, with the mixture being put into white basins, and covered with white cloth, usually old sheet, and bound round with string, then steamed for hours on end.

I must tell you of two incidents that happened while out on my walks after school, both during that first autumn. You will recall that the boy who was billeted with me had two sisters, they stayed in a house within the main village area, the rear of which faced onto a field across which I often walked on my way home.This particular evening as I approached the house I could see Ken, and some other boys, they were looking up at the window, and shouting at the girls standing in the window, as I drew closer, I could see that the girls were only wearing their undergarments, and the boys were enticing them to remove them, now although I did not join in the jibes, I did stop, and watch, and eventually the girls removed their clothing, I was more embarrassed than shocked because although I came from a mixed family I could not remember ever seeing my sisters in this state of undress, I do know that I ran. I said nothing of what had happened that evening to anyone, and can only think that the incident was not witnessed by anyone else, I hate to think what the outcome would have been had it been seen by any of the villagers.

The second incident, again happened on my way home from a walk, but this time I was carrying my trusty bow, and arrows, the ground was covered with a thin layer of snow, and was mid week following a shoot the previous Saturday. I was approaching a fence bordering a field when I spotted a pheasant in the grass at the end of the hedge. Keeping to one side of the bird, I walked up to the fence, and climbed on to the top, I stood on the top rail, and saw that I was only about seven or eight feet from it, I wondered why it did not run, but all I could think of was killing it. I loaded an arrow, and fired, it struck the bird high on the chest, and it died.

I jumped from the fence, picked up my prize, and ran home, there I had a shock, John had already arrived home, he took the bird from me, felt its body, and laughed. Apparantly it had been shot, and badly wounded during that previous shoot, and it had been lying in the grass pining away, it was quite emaciated, and of course no good for eating, I was only too pleased that I had put it out of its misery. It is worth noting that that was the only time I ever hit anything in all my outings with the bow, and was probably why nobody ever stopped me using it, they knew very well, the likely hood of my hitting anything, was zero!

CHAPTER 12

Winter

When I broke up for the Christmas holidays on completion of that autumn term, the snow lay quite thick everywhere, in fact the drifts were so deep in some of the lanes that snow ploughs had to be employed so that the farmhands could move about the estate. The weather in the north of Hampshire can be quite severe in winter, and considering I was only some forty miles or so from where I lived previously, it is difficult to believe that snow was rarely seen in the south of England.

Christmas came, and went, I suppose I must have had presents of some sort, but I cannot recall, all I do remember is having chicken, and Christmas pudding for a celebration lunch, I would imagine that was more than some children received in my old city which was still subject to continuous bombing.

During that winter, much of my spare time was spent within the confines of the house, and although there was little to do, the time appeared to pass quickly. The house was warm, and inviting, and the Webb family treated us boys as their own, with the old man telling us tales of his long life spent in the area, man, and boy, a hard life, but one he never seemed to regret, they were happy days.

Only one thing marred that happy existence, and that was the onset of what I now know to have been migraine, severe pain in the face, and head, when it affected me I would lay on the floor in front of the Aga with little relief until I was sent to bed. In those days nobody seemed to know what it was, the doctor being so far away, it was a question of a couple of aspirins, and get on with it, fortunately I did not get these too often, and it certainly did not effect my way of life too much.

Gradually the days began to get longer, and I could look forward to them getting warmer, but that is for later.

During the early part of the new year, the younger of Mrs. Webb's two sons, Victor, joined the army, he may well have been called up, but I really do not know he certainly left the house to go to war with little fuss, I found that difficult to comprehend, because of my own experience, and as an essential worker he need not have gone.

Another thing that happened at this time, which, to me was disastrous, but as it turns out was to be the commencement of a very new experience, a pleasant one I might add, and one which was to give me another insight into other aspects of living in the country.

The estate manager informed the Webb family they would have to move, apparently the cowman was leaving, and their house would be needed for his replacement, why he could not have had the house being vacated I do not know, but all the accomodation in the village was tied, and of course the landlord, the Hon. Henderson could move the occupants wherever he chose. We were to be moved to a cottage in the hamlet of Netherton in the valley below Faccombe, only about half a mile, but at the bottom of a very steep hill. The cottage had not been lived in for some years, so while the necessary repairs were being carried out it was felt that Ken, and I should be placed in someone elses care for a few weeks, we were duly despatched to an old lady living in a very small cottage within the main village area. When I say the cottage was small, it was small with a capital "S", the ceilings were so low that we could jump from the bedroom window onto the garden below without injury, and often did.

What a few weeks we had here, the old lady, her name I cannot remember, was the opposite to the Webb's in that she was untidy about the house, unkempt in her appearance, but having the most wonderful personality. The food was something else, as you will remember, normally we would be served plain, but wholesome fare, not here, we started the day with a large fried breakfast, lunch was cooked, as was the evening meal which invariably included roast potatoes, it was absolute heaven to us boys, but not to last if course because soon the house at Netherton was ready, and we were required to move back to the Webb household. From here on I cannot remember Ken being with me, I rather think he opted to stay with the old lady, I cannot say that I blame him. but for me the orderly Webb way of life was more to my liking

I must recall one incident that happened during that winter when the snow lay thick, us two boys were having a snowball fight, and for some reason Ken got my back up, usually he got the better of me because of his size, and bullying nature, but not in this instance. I had rolled some snow into a hard ball, threw it at him with as much force as I could muster, and caught him on the side of the neck splitting the skin, and making him bleed, I remember I was frightened at the time, but I need not have worried, little harm was done, and like most bullies he backed off, two brownie points to me!

Netherton consisted of the cottage where I was to live, and I think two others on the other side of the road which I believe were unoccupied, our's was adjacent to an old church yard, no church, but there were gravestones. A path led from the road, an area opened off to the right, and the first thing to be seen was a disused well. boarded over, and the whole covered in a large roof structure, on a little, and again to the right was the cottage. I must just say, that the well area mentioned would be the scene of a happening that would live in my memory for the rest of my life, but more of that later.

The entrance to the cottage faced the church yard, there was a small porch with a pitched roof, a common feature on most dwellings in this part of the country. Although the house was small, there was ample room for the family, and me, depleted as it was now, certainly not the comfort we had been used to, but it did not seem to worry the Webb's, I believe it was a case of accepting the inevitable. Gone was the wonderful Aga range, cooking was now carried out on an old, very small range, one of those that had to be kept clean with black lead polish, the food was still plain, but wholesome.

One thing which was different to the house in Faccombe, the garden, the one in the house we had moved from was large, but this was huge, and flanked the cottage on both sides, much overgrown, but a lot of hard work by the old man, John, and myself soon had the ground prepared ready for planting. Everything possible was planted to enable the family to be self sufficient, during the rest of my time here we were able to enjoy fresh food every day. One thing was a little more difficult, John had to bring the milk down from the farm each day after work, this was carried in a tapered enamel can complete with a lid nicknamed a "fanny", he would also, when available bring fresh butter to supplement the very meagre ration allowed to each person, he also brought eggs, although he did not have to fetch these for very long, the expanse of the ground surrounding the cottage allowed John to keep chickens, and once these were laying, eggs were no longer a problem. Another addition was a pig, the Ministry of Agriculture allowed each family to keep one, of which half had to be handed to the Ministry following slaughter. John built a pig sty at the end of the garden opposite to the site of the well, and in due course a small piglet arrived, a saddleback, so named because it was black with a wide white stripe around its middle, apparently they grew very fast, and had very little fat. So began my sojourn at Netherton, so much would be crammed into that last six months with this family, although at the time I was unaware that that was to be the case.

Life went on much it had done in Faccombe, much further to walk to school of course, I was thankful that the worst of the winter was now over, but my main concern at this time was the preparation for the entrance exam to grammar school. As the day approached, I wondered how I would get to the school where I was to sit the exam, I had been informed that I would be required to attend Andover Grammar School for the first paper at ten am. I need not have worried as it turns out because the Lady of the Manor informed the school that she would lay on a car to take me, and as good as her word on the appointed day her own limousine arrived to collect me complete with her chauffeur, you can imagine how I felt,

I had rarely been in a car, and here I was travelling like royalty. I was dropped at the school in Andover in plenty of time, but was informed by the driver that I had to make my own way back to Netherton when the exams were completed, promptly handed me some money to cover the bus fare, and drove off.

I was more than a little worried about getting back home, because although I had made the journey previously on a number of occasions, I had always been accompanied by an adult, that though was for later, firstly I had my exam papers to tackle. The exam went well, one paper before lunch, one after, lunch was of the packed variety which Mrs. Webb had prepared for me the night previous, I cannot recall what the sandwiches were, but could hazard a guess that they would have been cheese between thick slices of fresh bread. The exam over, I made my way to the bus station, the light was beginning to fail now, being February the days were still quite short, so I had the daunting prospect of arriving home in complete darkness. The bus took me as far as Hurstbourne Tarrant, and from there on it was "shanks' pony".

I remember that the night was very clear, just as well, no street lights here, just the moon, and the stars to light the way. Everything looked so different in the darkness, I do not think I was frightened, but it was more than a little spookey. I walked along the valley with wide expanses of grass to each side, occasionally a rabbit would scamper out of its burrow, or from behind a bush, they were still around in large numbers at this time, that dreadful killer mixamatosis, had not been heard of yet, and rabbits are notorious for their breeding capacity. As I branched right to go up the hill to Faccombe the darkness was overpowering, the road led up through a wood, and the trees overhung the road to a point where they touched at the top, this was quite disturbing for me, it was not just the darkness, but the sounds. Every kind of noise imagineable could be heard coming from the ground, the trees, and the sky, bats flew back, and forth, and occasionally a fox would cross my path, that was an experience I would not like to repeat, but at the same time probably said something about my character, in that it did not worry me unduly.

You may be forgiven for thinking what in heavens name is he doing in Faccombe after telling you of my move, yes, you have guessed it, I had forgotten that I had moved to Netherton, so had to turn left when reaching the village, go past the farm, and on down the hill to my new home. What the family thought about my memory lapse I do not recall, they only seemed interested in how I had got on with my exam.

The seasons are coming around again, so my intention now is to cover the period from now until I left the Webb's in that late summer of 1942 in one chapter, many things happened that I had not experienced before, and will try and keep them in some order.

CHAPTER 13

Final Thoughts

During that final Easter holiday, I again found myself working in the gardens of the Manor House, cleaning flower pots once more, but this time given additional tasks to do to relieve the monotony, such as staking the tomato plants in the greenhouses, hoeing, and weeding. I was being trusted, and that felt good, expectations were high in this nursery because of the quality demanded by the cook in the house, so you can imagine how I felt when I was allowed to carry out less menial tasks.

Back at Netherton, the garden was beginning to establish itself, and we were looking forward to early potatoes etc., the pig was putting on weight at an incredible rate, so he should have done judging by what he consumed each day, mostly potatoes, and all the scraps from the preparation of the vegetables, and a corn mash of some sort, all cooked in a very large iron pot which was kept continuously boiling on the stove, the cottage never seemed to be free of the smell of that pig food. When the feed was cooked, it was tipped into a large barrel kept to one side of the front door, when the pig needed feeding, a quantity would be scooped from the barrel, and transported down the garden to the pigs trough. That pig was almost human, he knew exactly when it was time to be fed, and would scream when the time approached, the food was not long in his trough, and once he had eaten it, would look at you as much to say "where is the rest".

In early summer, I learnt that I had passed my exams, and would be required to present myself at the Portsmouth Southern Secondary School for Boys, in Brockenhurst, in September, it is worth noting that it was renamed "Grammar" when we returned to Portsmouth after the war, the original school was destroyed by bombing, so was transferred to what was originally a first world war hospital in the New Forrest, another wonderful part of England.

That last summer was wonderful, a repeat of the previous one, and to me, not in the least bit boring, I had become a true person of the country, I even spoke like the locals, something that would make me the butt of jokes for a while when I joined my new school. I still had a few months before I was due to leave, so made my mind up to enjoy my time to the full.

I had heard that there was an old gallows on a hill along the valley towards Coombe, and asked John if he would take me there, he said that he would, but I needed to wait until he was free on a Saturday. Eventually came that day, and I was surprised to find that John had managed to borrow the Alice Chalmer tractor, it would seem that it was quite a way along the valley, terminating in a steep climb to the summit of the hill on which was the gallows, we would have to park the tractor, and walk to the site.

We saw no one as we drove along the valley, I say "we", John was driving, and I was standing on the rear platform leaning against the mudguard, quite a common practice, particularly if more than one farmhand had to go somewhere on the estate to collect a piece of equipment. The tractor was parked up, and we ascended the hill, some 1000 feet above sea level, so I was told, as we reached the brow, I could see what looked like a tree growing out of the ground at an angle, it was the trunk of a tree, stripped of its branches, and probably some ten feet in height, blackened with years of being exposed to the elements, and carved initials, and signs all over it. I remember I stood, and stared at what to me was an awesome sight silhouetted against the sky line, it was a warm sunny afternoon, but I could see it on a miserable day, with a crowd of onlookers all shouting for revenge against some poor soul about to be hung for *what* today would have been a minor offence, thank God that barbaric act no longer exists today.

That visit did not affect me any way, no nightmares, but it did live in my memory, so much so , that a few years ago I revisited that site in the company of my wife, but was dissapointed to find that it is now under the care of the National Trust, the hanging post had gone, and a tall ornate column erected in its place close to the original site. The view of the surrounding countryside is wonderful still, but the atmosphere created by that original gallows has sadly gone, when I stood on that hill as a boy I felt that I had been transported back in time.

Those long summer days were being savoured with more relish this time around because I was conscious of my impending departure from this mini paradise where I had been able to put behind me the trauma of the loss of my father, mainly due to the care, and understanding of my adopted parents, albeit temporary, I would think of them often in the coming years with a great deal of affection.

Before breaking up for the summer holidays I had to say my goodbyes to the two teachers, they had given me the incentive to try, and achieve a better life for the future, and I thanked them for that, many of the other children would be off home to their parents, so that would be the last I would see of them, as children, there was no great emotional parting, just "cheerio", I though would be staying a while.

I had thought that my last summer here would fly by, but it did not, for one thing I discovered more of the valley area of the estate, the dryer mentioned previously was quite close to the cottage, this enabled me to spend more time there during the harvest, that does not mean that I neglected my favourite pass time of following the combines, and trying to catch rabbits, we were still able to enjoy rabbit stew following a successful day in the fields.

Most of the children as I said were away from the village for the summer recess, so the church had to do without a choir for a while, in fact I remember I did not attend for service again that summer, most remiss of me, but as I previously said, I was not aware of any true Christian belief at that time.

Some of my time was spent working in the Manor House garden, I recall one of the tasks I had to carry out, was encasing the desert fruits such as pears, apples, peaches etc. in small muslin bags so that they did not fall to the ground before they were ready to be picked for use in the house, most of this fruit was grown along wires attached to the walls of the cottage garden, often I was tempted to help myself, but my earlier encounter with Mrs. Henderson, and the law, prevented me from doing so.

I was to witness one more act common to the countryside at this time, the slaughter of John's pig, at the end of that summer it weighed in at around twenty score pounds, apparently John could tell by looking at it that the time was right, and date was made for the vet to visit, and carry out the necessary slaying. On the appointed day the vet arrived in the early afternoon, it would appear that some other business had prevented him coming in the morning as arranged, this annoyed John because what he had planned to do with the pig had now gone by the board, there was little he could do about it so had to accept that some of the work would have to be carried over to the following day.

The pig had to be led from its pen down to the site of the old well at the other end of the garden, I will never forget that pigs reluctance to walk that fifty yards or so, I am sure he knew what was about to happen. He was finally standing under the roof of the well on the boards that covered the top of the well, the vet put the gun to his head between the eyes, fired, it was all over, and he keeled over on to his side.

Although I was close to being sick at what was about to take place, I just stood, and watched, spellbound by a seeming barbaric act. The vet cut the animals throat, and there was a deluge of blood which ran down between the boards, and into the well below. A rope was thrown over the roof rafters, tied around the back legs of the pig, and John, *and* the vet hauled it up until it was hanging vertically, that was the end of the vets work, he said his goodbyes, and went on his way.

I was puzzled by what John did next, he lit a bonfire, and, when it was going well he made a torch, lit it from the fire, made his way back to where the pig was hanging, and ran it over the whole body to burn off the hair, very simple, and effective. He next slit the stomach down its whole length, and removed all the internal organs into a small bath, and presented them to Mrs. Webb. For those of you who do not know, every single piece of a pig except perhaps its tail, and eyes can be consumed, and what the good lady had to do was to clean the intestines right through, and prepare the liver, kidneys etc. The intestines would be boiled for many hours before they were ready to eat, quite honestly I could not stand the sight of them, let alone eat them, the liver though was quite different, absolutely delicious, and to this day I think it is the best of livers to eat.

The carcase of the pig hung under the well roof until the following day, I went to my bed that night wondering if any animals would attack it, and gorge on it, but when I awoke the following morning, and looked out of my window, there it was, just as it had been left the evening before. John's task this day was to divide the carcase, first into two halves, you will remember that one had to go to the Ministry of Agriculture, the other he cut into suitably sized sections for use in the house, much of it, mainly the bacon joints were to be salted down to supplement the meat ration over the winter months, the rest was stowed in the larder, no fridges in those days, even though it was only half a carcase, it was still a substantial amount of meat.

The time finally came for me to say my goodbyes, they were not sad because for the Webb's I was just a boarder really, although I was aware that there was a great deal of affection shown to me in their quiet unassuming way, I am sure that John knew that he had been a father figure to me. My small bag had been packed for me, all my clothes, such as they were, were clean, and I was given a packed lunch for my journey. I cannot recall how I arrived at Andover station, or whether I was accompanied by my mother, I do know that the train I boarded was to take me to

Southampton where I had to change for the connection to Brockenhurst, and there would be met by someone from my new school.

The memories of my brief spell with the Webb family in Faccombe, and Netherton will live with me for ever. I was given such an insight into country life in all its aspects, an appreciation of nature which has given me so much pleasure throughout my life, but for the war, I might never have experienced those sights, sounds, and smells of a countryside fast diminishing in the present day. This wonderful family has now sadly passed on, so I cannot let them really know what the time spent with them actually meant to me, somehow I believe they knew.

CHAPTER 14

Coterie

The journey to Brockenhurst was uneventful, but exciting in that following the change at Southampton, the train which was to take me to my destination was drawn by a Lord Nelson class engine, one which I had never before seen. I cannot give you the wheel set up by which engines are identified, I was never that much of an enthusiast, suffice to say that it was extremely large, and powerful. Apparantly these engines were on regular runs to Bournemouth, as I recall the livery was green, black, and with a great deal of polished brass, and copper, the sight, and sound of these engines drawing into the station was wonderful, sadly missed today of course because the only time steam engines can be enjoyed now is on the privately owned lines, and the engines seen are of the smaller variety.

I rather think that we were advised of the connection at Southampton because a good many boys seemed to waiting there, and on arrival at Brockenhurst we were met by one of the staff, and taken to the school just a short walk away. The school was set back off the main road, with an approach road running between two large expanses of grass, and consisted of a series of single storey timber buildings. We were assembled in the hall, and according to preference allocated lodgings, either in a hostel or a private residence, I had opted for the latter because of my previous experience with the Webb family, and as I thought, a dislike of communal living, this as you will see was a big mistake.

I was to take up residence with another boy, his name I cannot remember, in a house quite close to the school, owned by a couple who had no children of there own, a recipe for disaster if ever there was. They were nice enough people, fed us well, and kept us clean, but had no understanding of the young, and quite intolerant of even the smallest misdemeanour.

That first morning at my new school was a little chaotic. Following assembly we were given a talk by the head master, a Mr. Jones, Welsh of course, on the discipline required during school hours. I remember he came bouncing into the hall with gown flowing, and mortar-board on his head, something I had never seen before, that though was to become a familiar site because all the staff wore gowns, but most carried their mortar-boards. When the head had finished, and the rest of the pupils had dispersed to their various class rooms, the new entry were split into three classes of approximately thirty boys in alphabetical order, A, B, C, this was for one term only, in the January following the xmas holiday we were expected to sit an exam, and we would then be graded according to merit.

I was to be in the A class, and my form master was to be a Mr. Shackleton, "Shacks" to the boys, he was also to teach me chemistry. He was a rather scruffy individual in a sports jacket, and cord trousers, of heavy build, slicked down hair, and glasses, apparently he had been a pilot in the first world war, had been shot down over France, and quite badly burned. He was to be a good friend to me, he was an official of an organisation in Portsmouth that helped orphans of the war, I had lost my father so he thought he would help me in any way he could. He was about the only master who on occasions did not wear his gown, mind you it was rather the worst for wear, and he always seemed to have difficulty in keeping it in place because of the tatters, he never carried his mortar board, perhaps he did not have one.

We were all given time tables, which included many subjects that I had never encountered, such as French, Science, this would be split into chemistry, and physics in the second year. Art, Sport, as well as English which would cover language, and literature. Maths which would include Geometry, and Algebra, Civics which at the time was the study of Local, and Central Government, all that I had covered previously was arithmetic, English, and general knowledge, so some changes were about to hit me.

It was after reading the time table that I felt I was joining an "exclusive circle", one of the few, privileged to be able to study under such an august band of academics.

Class periods were of forty minutes duration, three in the morning, three in the afternoon, and where sport or science occurred they were of two periods together. This made good sense because the playing field was about half a mile away on a hill, and practical laboratory work had to be carried out in Brockenhurst County School, again some distance from my school, this school had great facilities which was more than could be said for the playing field, atop a hill with no changing rooms, it was horrendous in the winter changing ready to play football.

Somehow we all settled into the routine, and except for science, and sports all lessons were taken in one classroom, with the relevant masters coming to us. Lunch was served in the hall where we sat about twelve to a table, I say served, but in fact one of us had to go just outside the hall where there were hatches to the kitchen, here we would be handed large dishes containing whatever was on the menu for that day, never a choice on the main course, just good wholesome food. The sweet however was a different matter, there was a choice, but the likelyhood of you getting your preference was very remote, that is until I made a friend of the cook. I remember that she was a very small lady, quite fat, and decidedly ugly, and abrupt when she spoke to you, but for some reason she took a shine to me, so I would tap the hatch before lunch was served, she would tell me what was on offer for sweet, and I would book what I thought the lads would like, you can imagine I was popular, it continued for a very long time, and there was only a problem if the cook was not in the kitchen for some reason.

I know that I am going to have great difficulty in putting everything in chronological order for the next four year period, but will endeavour to make the memory work harder to achieve the end result.

CHAPTER 15

First Term

Class work this first term was fairly routine, except where I had to embrace new subjects. Science I liked because it was interspersed with practical experiments, general Mathematics, problems etc. were not new, so that I coped with, Goemetry I found no problem with, as far as I was concerned, it was just an extention of drawing. Algebra I found very difficult, but when I eventually got the hang of it I realised that you could solve a theorem, and other problems much simpler with the use of this method. Art class became one of my all time favourites, I was naturally good at drawing, so rather excelled at that, the master, his name I cannot remember, was a talented water colour artist, and tried to pass his knowledge on to his pupils, some of us succeeded, and a great deal of pleasure was to be had in another direction because of this, and I will relate that later.

During this term, sport consisted of football, and cross country running, I had never participated in either of these before, but say that I enjoyed both. I became reasonably skilled at football finding that my best position was that of right half, I could only kick with my right foot, and was more of a defender than a forward, the term "right half" is never used today, the formation on the field often changes to suit the opposition. Although I had never ran seriously before, I was quite fit, and found that cross country running suited me well, and soon became good enough to represent my house. Each boy was allocated a "house", there were four, each of a different colour, mine was blue, and you kept that colour throughout your time at school.

During my time at the Southern I regularly represented my house at all sports, but was, by far, most successful at cross country. Those four years saw three boys dominate the main events, Ron. Carrol green house, Brian Edwards, house I cannot recall, and myself, and except for only one occasion that I can remember, the order of finish was Ron Carrol, myself, and Brian Edwards, try as I did I could never outstrip Ron. Brian was never a very charitable loser, he was a natural athlete, and excelled at all sports, in fact when he finished his time at the Southern he signed professional forms for Portsmouth Football Club, but never appeared on a regular basis, I have no idea what became of him, but I suppose he must have moved to a lesser club where he would be able to play more regularly.

Such was how my time was taken up during school hours, but what of my life in my new home, not so good. The nights were drawing in of course, so I could not stay out of doors for too long, and there was homework every night of the week. and at week ends, I believe I could have coped well had there been some understanding from the couple I was billeted with, but things were so different from my life with the Webb's, I began to miss my father again, and would often wake up in the night somewhat disturbed, and if I tried to discuss my problem it was just passed off as if nothing.

The problem was exacerbated further when I on occasion wet the bed, something I had never done in my life, and you can imagine, at my age it troubled me a great deal, particularly as it angered my guardians so much, and still no attempt was made to solve the underlying cause. Things came to head about two thirds the way into that first term, I found out that an approach had been made to the school to have me moved from my present billet by the start of the new term. This in no way worried me until I was told I would be moved to a hostel, you will remember that I spoke of my distaste of communal living although I had no real experience of that way of life, my fears were quite unfounded however, but I was not to know that until I was installed in my new home following the Christmas break, one which I did not overly enjoy because of the worry about the forthcoming move.

The trauma of home life at that time did not stop me pursuing activities out of doors that had been of interest to me during my stay with the Webb's. The New Forrest is a wonderful part of the country, totally different from the area around Faccombe, in that a river ran through Brockenhurst, and much of the land beyond was heath where ponies, and cattle ran freely. The river area was my favourite, and in particular a section where it widened into a small lake surrounded by trees, one of which had a platform built in the branches for diving from, I never used this for the simple reason that I could not swim, something I never learnt to do, I doubt there were any baths in the area open during the war even if I had the inclination to learn.

Not being able to swim did not discourage me from one activity which, when I think of it now, was rather foolhardy. There was a stretch of the river which had trees on each bank, and several of us boys would collect at this spot at the weekend to cross the river like monkeys. One tree in particular was found to be strong enough, and pliable enough for you to climb to the top, and it would almost bend to the opposite bank, and allow you to drop to the ground. I was small, and light in weight so I would often have to jump the branch up, and down to enable me to get close enough to the ground, and drop to my feet safely, I was always scared, but had to brave it out in front of my mates.

I must tell you of one ritual that took place each Friday when school had finished for the weekend."Shacks", the chemist, lived in Portsmouth, and as such, was allowed a petrol allowance for his vehicle, a rather old motorbike, and, come rain or shine he would ride it home to Portsmouth for the weekend. You will recall I spoke of the approach road to the school, it was here that it appeared that half the school would line both sides of the road, and await the arrival of "Shacks". He would immerge from the school astride his trusty steed dressed in an old raincoat, scarf thrown around his neck, with on his head his old leather flying helmet complete with goggles. All the boys would cheer, and shout "good old shacks" to which he never seemed to take offence, just a wave of his hand, and he was gone, memories such as this can be savoured over, and over.

I had almost forgot to tell you of the new church choir I joined soon after my arrival in Brockenhurst, the name of the church I do not remember, but I believe there was only one C of E church in the village so any of you familiar with the area may know which one I am talking about. The church was unimpressive in appearance inside, and out, but the choir was something else in that there were lady members, something I had never seen before. Us choir boys were dressed in the familiar cassock, gown, and ruff, the men were dressed the same, but no ruff, the females, women, and young girls wore bright coloured gowns, and carried mortar boards, and there were so many members that the choir stalls on each side of the aisle were full, you can imagine this made for a magnificent sight during the services, and I can say that the sound was just as good. I enjoyed my time with this choir, short lived though it was to be, and looking back I rather think that some comfort was drawn from it during this most difficult of times. I do not think that I had the true belief of a Christian even then, and in any case, going to church was rather frowned upon by a good many of my class mates, so you invariably said little of your visits to church each Sunday.

That first term finally came to an end, and we broke up for the Christmas holidays, and, although I came back to Portsmouth I have no recollection of where I stayed, it was probably with my grandmother who was then living in Lake Road, or what I did during that break except for one party I attended.

You will remember my reference to Mr. Shackleton's charity work on behalf of war orphans, and before we broke up he asked me to call on him at his home in St. Ronans Road, in Southsea, a road which was flanked on one side by a school, little did any of us know that the Southern would occupy that very school on its return to Portsmouth after the war, as I said earlier, the original premises were destroyed in the blitz. I duly arrived at Shacks house on the appointed day, and on entering the porch to ring the bell, noticed that mounted diagonally across one of the side walls was an aircraft propeller. On being ushered in, I questioned him about it, apparently it was salvaged from his old aircraft when he was shot down in the first world war! The reason he wanted to see me was to give me details of a party he was organising, and he requested that I attend, I accepted, and duly attended on the appointed day, and had a wonderful time, I believe I attended the following year, but no more, I was probably getting too old.

That man was kindness itself, what I would call a true Christian, he was one of the masters to have a lasting affect on me, I shall never forget him. Later I will tell of something he said the first time he ever took the class I was in for chemistry, a profound statement, meant to be taken most seriously, but to us boys, it was at the time highly amusing.

That first holiday drew to a close, and I looked forward to my return to school, with, as you would expect, some trepidation.

Arnwood Towers

The Full Complement

*I acknowledge that the Davies family allowed me to use photos etc
from their peronal archives.*

The Choir

I am standing at the back, right hand, and Bert is sitting in the front row, second from right.

In Aid of Lymington Borough
SALUTE THE SOLDIER
Variety Entertainment at the W.I. Hall Hordle on
SATURDAY, APRIL 29th at 7.30 p.m.

SONG & CHORUS	Hordle Players
" A BOB IN THE POUND "	
PIANOFORTE SOLO	Mrs. A. A. Davies, A.T.C.L.
SONGS (Selected)	Mrs. Gale
SONGS ,,	Mr. F. Wright

PLAY
"THE BLOATERS"
(By Ella Adkins)

MRS. BROWN		Trevor West
GEORGIE		S. Reay
EMILY	HER	R. Dopson
HAROLD	CHILDREN	D. Tolfree
BILL		B. Draper
MRS. MUGGINS		— R. Moore —
ROSE		H. Smith
BASIL		G. Oxley

Produced by MR. R. R. DAVIES, B.sc.

SONG (Selected)	Miss Learmount
DUET ,,	Masters L. Broad & R. Farrar
PIANOFORTE SOLO	Mrs. A. A. Davies, A.T.C.L.

PLAY
"ORANGE BLOSSOM"
(By Philip Johnson)

MR. DUCKWORTH	Lily Brampton
MRS. DUCKWORTH	Rose Williams
GLAD DUCKWORTH	Elizabeth Nelson
AUNTIE LOLA	Nellie Renyard
AUNTIE LOTTIE	Gardyne Ballard
AMY FOSTER	Phyllis Rose
FRED ASHFORD	Hetty Beale

Produced by MRS. COLIN GRAY

SONGS (Selected)	Mrs. Gale
SONGS ,,	Mr. F. Wright
DUET ,,	Masters L. Broad & R. Farrar
SONGS ,,	Miss Learmount
PIANOFORTE SOLO	Mrs. A. A. Davies, A.T.C.L.

NATIONAL ANTHEM

8th June, 1946

TO-DAY, AS WE CELEBRATE VICTORY, I send this personal message to you and all other boys and girls at school. For you have shared in the hardships and dangers of a total war and you have shared no less in the triumph of the Allied Nations.

I know you will always feel proud to belong to a country which was capable of such supreme effort; proud, too, of parents and elder brothers and sisters who by their courage, endurance and enterprise brought victory. May these qualities be yours as you grow up and join in the common effort to establish among the nations of the world unity and peace.

George R.I

PORTSMOUTH EDUCATION COMMITTEE.

SOUTHERN SECONDARY SCHOOL FOR BOYS.

Head Master: G. B. H. JONES, M.C., M.A. (Cantab.), Barrister-at-Law.

Report for period from _September 1945_ to _February 1946._

Form _IVB._ Name _R. G. Moore._ Age _15 : 4_

Subject			Marks	Maxima	Form Averages	Position	Remarks
Scripture	...	...	19	50	21	21	
English	...	...	139.	300	150	23.	
History	...	...	72	150	73	17.	
Geography	...	...	79	150.	85.	12.	
French	...	...	142	300.	149.	17.	
Latin	...	...					
Mathematics	...	...	289	400	196	1.	
Physics	...	...	140	300	130.	9.	
Chemistry	...	..	134	300	127.	12.	
Art	...	...	116	150.	89.	5.	
Manual Instruction		...					
Music	...	...					
TOTAL		...	1130.				

Physical Training ....

Position in Form _5th._

Absences _40._

Times late _0._

Detentions _t._

Games ....

No. of Boys in Form _30._

Form Master _G. Thomas_

REMARKS :

1. Conduct : _Good._

2. Work : _Good but uneven. hindered by absences._

Head Master _G. B. H. Jones_

Signature of parent or guardian : _

Date _25th February, 1946._

DEEPLY REGRET TO REPORT DEATH OF YOUR HUSBAND ON WAR SERVICE

Royal Oak wreath

While the Leander-class frigate H.M.S. Apollo was on patrol in the area of Scapa Flow, one of the ship's officers took the opportunity of laying a wreath over his father's grave, the battleship H.M.S. Royal Oak.

Lieut. Ted Moore's father was a Royal Marine, who joined the Royal Oak just a month before she was sunk at Scapa Flow in September 1939.

Duplicate of Inspector's Certificate issued on 2nd July 1940

Ref. D.N.A.—Wills **1888**
1939

CERTIFICATE
OF THE INSPECTOR OF SEAMEN'S WILLS.

ADMIRALTY, *the* 26th *day of* May 1950

IN pursuance of Act of Parliament 28th and 29th Vic., cap 111, and Order in Council 28th December, 1865, which provide that the Naval Assets of any deceased COMMISSIONED OFFICER, WARRANT OFFICER, PENSIONER, CIVILIAN, or OTHER PERSON mentioned therein, belonging to or having belonged to a Naval Establishment, when not exceeding One Hundred Pounds, may be paid without Letters of Administration or Probate of Will being taken out, if the claimant's right has been duly investigated and allowed by the Inspector of Seamen's Wills, whose Certificate sanctioning payment is to have the same force and effect as, and the payment on its authority be as valid and conclusive as if made under, Probate or Letters of

Administration; I HEREBY CERTIFY THAT THE APPLICATION OF....................

Now Residing at :— Mrs Florence Ada Moore

residing at 2, White Cloud Cottage, Highland Road, Southsea, Hampshire

claiming as lawful widow

the Effects of the late Leonard George Moore a Marine Royal Marines Reg. No. Po/ 20158 ....who died intestate........................ on the 14th October 1939

has been duly verified and attested as prescribed by the Order in Council, and the statements therein appearing to be true, that the said Claimant is entitled to receive what is due on account of the deceased in the Naval Department (it not exceeding ONE HUNDRED POUNDS), in order to administer the same according to Law.

A. J. Hawkins

for Inspector of Seamen's Wills

NOTE

This Certificate should be carefully kept and not destroyed or mislaid.

Now Residing at:
66, Bredenbury Crescent,
Paulsgrove,
Portsmouth.

Description of Effects for which this Certificate is granted.	Amount.			Mode and Date of Payment.
	£	s.	d.	
Residue of Wages	—	13	1	By Postal Draft No. 78248 dated 8/7/40
Naval Prize Money	4	4	—	Ruby Navy Bill No 28412 dated 22/6/50

HMS Royal Oak

Photo courtesy of the National Museum of the Royal Navy

25.08.03 – 31.08.03

THE WAY WE WERE:

Howzat for a photograph?

Ron Brown this
week runs stories
of cricket teams
and railway lines

Bert Shott, who is 83, sent me three excellent photographs of the Portsmouth Southern Secondary School football and cricket teams from his days of youth there in the 1930s.

The other two will eventually appear in our various nostalgia features, but today we are publishing the earliest of the school cricket team in 1932. The three masters at the back are Mr Ogden, Mr Winter and Mr Stocks, while the headmaster sitting in the middle is Dr Collier.

Bert tells me the pictures were taken outside the main entrance to the school, which was a victim of bombing during the second world war, but the girls' school remains as Priory School. The school hours for girls was different to the boys – this was done to discourage unseemly fraternising.

Bert has provided a long list of the masters, and their nicknames. Mr GBH Jones was the headmaster in 1935 – yes, he was known as GBH.

*Have included this cutting from the "News", Portsmouth, because
Mr Ogden and Mr Stocks were still on the staff when I joined the
Southern in September, 1942*

Article Courtesy of The News, Portsmouth

CHAPTER 16

Arnwood Towers

I believe I arrived at Arnwood the day previous to starting the second term of my first year, but I am not certain of that, I would certainly have had to be met at Sway station, because the walk from the station to the hostel was about a mile, and a half, and I would in no way have found it without help, it may well be that I attended school that day, and travelled to Arnwood with all the other boy's who were billeted there. For the foreseeable future I would have to walk that road twice a day on my way to the station for the journey to school at Brockenhurst.

Mr. R. R. Davies, my maths master, ran the hostel with his wife, a fact I was unaware of until my arrival, rather strange on reflection, because some of the boy's in my class lived there, just goes to show what a loner I was up to this point in time.

As a priority when I arrived, I was introduced to the staff, Mrs.Davies, her sister Mrs. Gadsby, her husband was in the R.A.F. I cannot remember ever having seen him, two prefects, one was Monty Vinyl, he eventually became head of school, the other escapes me, and the cook, later I would meet the housekeeper, and her husband, they lived in the bungalow/cottage which was situated to the right as you entered the property, I believe they were part of the original staff attached to the house, Mr. Stead, an English master was so often at the house, I thought he was a member of staff, it was only recently I found out that in fact he ran a similar establishment called Rhinefield House, two other important residents were the Davies' two daughters, more of them, and Mr. Stead later.

When I first took sight of the house, it was through two very large piers on which must have hung a pair of impressive metal gates, theses would have been removed to a munitions factory to aid the war effort. The house was on the right as you approached up a shingle drive, there were several garages/stables one of which housed a limousine, it was mounted on timber blocks with the wheels removed, that would very definitely not be used for the duration! The house, although a mansion, was not a stately home, the drive continued round to the right to the front entrance, in front of which were extensive lawns complete with sundry beds containing shrubs, and large conifer trees, this then was to be my new home.

I believe there were fifty three of us boy's billeted here, sleeping in dormitories, eight, seven, six to a room depending on the size, all the rooms were on one landing, as were the bathrooms, only two as I recall, these caused a bit of a headache mornings, and evenings, with the rush to get ready for school. All rooms had names, the first room I was allocated was Oswold Partridge, one of the larger with eight beds, I say the first, because later I was moved to the smallest, for reasons I will go into later.

The name "Arnwood Towers" derived from Arnwood the name of the house, and "Towers" from the two towers/follies built in the grounds, the whole of the structure of the house, and towers was of concrete, quite revolutionary when built, one of the towers was about fifty feet, and the other in excess of three hundred feet.

The towers were out of bounds to all of us boy's except if we were accompanied by one of the staff, or a prefect, the reason being, they were too dangerous. The smaller one I visited on more than one occasion, but the taller, only once, for a start it took about half an hour to ascend the spiral staircase to the top, and it was not very often that any one of the staff wanted the climb. The larger tower had three hundred, and sixty five steps representing the days of the year, and twelve rooms for the months if the year, these rooms had huge windows from floor to ceiling, and were completely open, whether they were ever glazed, I have no idea, but you can imagine how dangerous it would have been to go too near to the edge, particularly near the top. The view from that top room was magnificent with the forest on one side, and the Solent, and Isle of White on the other.

As I have previously said, the house was not a mansion, but was large, and proved very adequate for the numbers now in residence. On the ground floor was a large dining room which doubled up as a prep room in the evenings, after we had finished our high tea at about six o'clock, the homework would be overseen by one of the prefects, and was of a compulsory two hour duration, the prefect invariably would be studying for his future at university. Next to this room was the boys lounge area, another large area where we could relax, and read or play board games, it also had another use which proved popular with a few of the lads, including myself. Some evenings after prep, Mr Davies would read aloud from popular adventure novels such as The Three Muscateers, or one of Raphael Sabatini's, they would sometimes go on for weeks, wonderful, he would make the books come alive with his different voices, there is nothing quite like listening to someone reading aloud in this manner, the scene being painted so well you could almost smell it.

Another room was laid out purely for games, a three quarter billiard table, a table tennis table (pingpong), and numerous smaller tables, and chairs for board games, chess being the one we were most encouraged to play, hobbies such as stamp collecting were also pursued in this area. You will have noticed that I said "billiard" table, and not snooker, as far as I can recall there were no snooker balls, so we had to content ourselves with billiards, in my opinion a much underrated game requiring a great deal of skill.

One very large room on the ground floor was out of bounds unless invited to enter, Mrs. Davies' sitting room. This had glazed doors from the corridor, the floor was of polished strip planking, on two levels, it dropped to a lower level at the front of the house, where French doors led out on to the drive, and the lawns beyond. This sitting room was pleasantly furnished, and included a grand piano, this was used mainly by Mrs Davies, an accomplished musician, and Mr. Stead who often assisted with the choir, and orchestra, more of those later.

I have dwelt briefly on the first floor bedrooms, but will more fully cover those later, I do remember one oddity on one corner of the first floor, a small tower room, would have made a wonderful study, perhaps it originally was.

There was one other small area on the ground floor which was crucial to maintaining one of the rules of the house, the shoe cleaning area, long, and narrow with a door leading from the house at one end, and at the other end a door leading out on to the drive, along one complete wall was a concrete bench, I rather think that this was used for cleaning birds or rabbits following a shoot etc. it certainly made an ideal bench for shoe cleaning.

Everyone was expected to have clean footwear to go to school, and to that end a roster was drawn up with one boy appointed to cover the inspection of shoes each day for one week, he would stand at the exit door, and we would have to pass through this rather narrow room to get past him, if your shoes did not come up to the required standard you would have to go back, and polish them again. You can imagine the problems this caused if several boys were trying to clean their shoe for the second time, we were invariably late getting away in the mornings, with always a rush to be on the road for the station to catch the only available train to get us to Brockenhurst on time..

Below the ground floor were enormous cellars with large concrete benches, one can only suppose that these were the wine cellars, if they were, there was no sign of any on our arrival. These areas were given over as workshops for making wooden toys for local orphans, model making etc. I spent many hours here, it was my first real taste of woodworking, and was to be the foretaste of my first job on leaving school.

The furnishing of the bedrooms was standard throughout, single iron bedsteads with a matress, pillow, sheets, blankets, and overlay, no duvets in those days, each of us had a small locker where all our worldly goods would be kept. All the windows had unlined curtains hung under wooden painted pelmets, and from one of these windows in each room was hung a roll up ladder for access to the ground outside should there have been a fire. Regular drills were carried out as you would expect, with most of us hoping we were on the first floor when the fire bell rang so that we could experience the climb down the ladder.

I hope that you now have a fair idea of how the house would have looked like in those far off days, an absolute haven for those of us who were to spend the rest of the war here. You may wonder how the house got its name, I rather think that it was always Arnwood, but the names of the rooms probably thought up by Mr.Davies, I really do not know, I do know, because I was told on arrival there, that all the names appertained to caracters from the book by Capt F. Marryatt. "The Children of The New Forrest" this I was encouraged to read to fully understand the story which was set in the time of the civil war in England 1647. The house, Arnwood was the residence of a cavalier called Col. Beverley, he had four children, Edward 13, Humphry 12, Alice 11, and Edith 8. There was also the Colonels servant, 60 years old Jacob Armitage, and another old retainer named Benjamin, he was rather weak of interlect, there was one other servant in the house, a Benjamin White. On the estate the verdera was Oswold Partridge, with Mr. Heatherstone, the forest agent for Cromwell, although his loyalty lay with King Charles I.

Why Marryat should deviate from his usual tales of the sea, I doubt that we shall ever know, one thing is certain, this is a cracking good yarn, and should be read by all young boys, I rather think that most girls would also enjoy it.

This then was how the rooms became named, Edward, Humphry, Beverley, Armitage, Benjamin, Partridge, and Heatherstone, I will though admit, that I may be mistaken in the number of rooms, and the names taken up for use, however, I have no doubt that those of you choosing to read this, will, in your minds, correct my text.

CHAPTER 17

Second Term

That first morning leaving Arnwood to go to school was quite an eye opener, we were awakened from sleep by the clanging of a bell, we were not exactly anxious to leap out of bed, but each room had a head boy, and he was responsible for ensuring that we set to, had our wash, and generally dressed ready for school before going for breakfast. This varied from day to day, cornflakes, porridge, eggs, sausage etc. with always bread, and margarine, and tea. Some things we did not like of course, invariably you were able to swap dishes on different days, if you could not, then you would have to fill up on bread, and margarine, when it was your turn to have what your partner did not like, you ended up with double helpings! The tea was served in large enamel jugs from which you helped yourself into tin mugs, I noticed that there were always two large jugs, and one small, the large ones were sweetened, the small was not, I had always had my tea sweet, but it took so long for the large jugs to go around that I decided to try the unsweetened, I liked it, and since that time have drunk nothing else, so very few boys liked it unsweetened, that there was always plenty in the small jug.

Each week, four or five boys had to do kitchen duty, this entailed laying, and clearing the tables at meal times, and peeling sufficient potatoes on the Saturday to last the weekend. There did not seem to be too much objection to this chore once a term, except perhaps the peeling of the "spuds", it did seem an endless task.

Breakfast over, it was "clean your teeth time", and on the road for the hike to the station, about one, and a half miles, very pleasant when the weather was fine, but sometimes we would get caught in a shower, and would arrive at school looking more than a little dishevelled. Most days Mr. Davies would accompany us, and most boys would avoid walking near him if they could, I though did not mind, he was to become another father figure to me. I remember that in the winter he wore large leather gauntlet gloves, and if there was anyone not conducting himself in the proper manner, he would remove a glove, and soundly clip you round the ears, because of this his sobriquet became "clack".

Mr. Davies' initials were R. R., and he had a brother whose initials were S.G., both taught maths, and at school were referred to as R. R., and S. G., but I only experienced R. R. in class.

I have great difficulty in remembering who taught which subjects, some however do stand out in the memory, but the reason for that is sometimes a little obscure. My art tutor I cannot remember, only that he taught me for four years, a subject so enjoyed, that the appreciation has stayed with me for all my life. There were several masters teaching English, and that first term I had the dubious pleasure of being taught be a minister of the church, whether he ever preached I cannot say, he appeared to teach full time, and out of school time he played trumpet in the school orchestra, and very good he was to, the only problem was, that whenever a public concert was performed, you could be sure that "Trumpet Voluntary" would appear on the programme. Only one thing springs to mind when I recall him teaching, if he was not at the blackboard writing, and wished to talk to you, he would stand leaning against the front of his desk, both hands in his pockets, and as us boys say "play pocket billiards".

Mr. Shackleton "shacks" as previously said, taught chemistry, in his rough, and ready way he imparted the subject in a way that kept our interest, and most did quite well at it, remembering the formulae was perhaps difficult, but the practical work more than made up for that. The first lesson with him, and his very first words following his introduction were as follows, with each word being punctuated with his hands, "You pour the liquid this way, and everything is fine, you pour it that way, bang! and we are trying to dig enough pieces out of the ceiling to make a decent funeral", a graphic way to instill care when dealing with chemicals.

Only one other master comes to mind that first year, Mr. Tilney "Tish" as he was known by, he taught French, I had enough problems coping with English, particularly because it now included literature, let alone trying to learn a new language. He was a brilliant linguist, but was hopeless at teaching other people, he was a very caring person, and a regularly attended church, something that would be exploited as I will recall later, just to look at him you knew instinctively that he would come in for a lot of stick from the pupils, he wore very heavy dark rimmed glasses, had a rather large wort on one cheek, and quite often wore his mortar board, poor old "Tish".

That first week back after the Christmas recess was mostly taken up with exams to determine where we would be placed for the rest of that first year, the results were known very quickly, and the classes were allocated in order of merit, I passed high enough to stay where I was, in the "A" class, something I was pleased about, because some of the work I was undertaking I had never before attempted, and that routine pattern established in that first term I wanted to carry on through my time at the "Southern", that though was not the way it would be as you will find out.

I must just mention the periods set aside for Physical Education, one per week, and consisting of two whole periods together, there were never any exercises as such, only the pursuit of whatever games or athletics were allocated for the season of the year, and during this second term it was to be football, and cross country running.

The running was fine, in that we could change into our kit in the confines of the school, and set off on the allocated route, usually a round trip of three or four miles. The course always went across country, and traversed all obstacles, up, and down hills, and across streams etc. on our return, more often than not because of the time of the year, we were covered in mud which had to be washed off, usually under cold water, never seemed to do us any harm though.

When football was the order of the day, it was quite a different matter, the pitches, such as they were, were some way from the school, no bus to transport us there, it was "shanks' pony", walking in other words ,and no weather ever stopped the pursuit of PE. These pitches, would you believe, were on the top of a hill, all adding to the fun of trying to learn the skills of "footer", there were no changing facilities, rain, snow, or shine you changed in the open, I cannot remember that there were any complaints, I suppose we did not know any different.

This then was how we learnt our athletic skills, nothing was taken too seriously, well not by many of the boys at any rate, but myself along with just a few others wanted to excel, so we took a more solemn approach, and competed with much enthusiasm, I have always maintained that the more adroit you become at any physical pastime, the more you will enjoy it, I had better not say too much on that score, my family will say I am on my soap box again!

Back at Arnwood, the weather limited our outside activities most of the time particularly in the evenings, because homework took up most of the time, and if you did manage to finish well within the allocated time, it was inevitably too dark to venture outside, however the weekends more than made up for that.

Before going into detail of our outside recreation, I must recall my room allocation during that first term at Arnwood because it is relevant to something which was to take place during this term each year. You will recall that I was placed in one of the larger rooms viz: Oswold Partridge, occupied by eight boys, not a good introduction to communal living, not only was I the smallest there, but in the language of today, I was the least "street wise" I did on occasion wet the bed, so you can imagine what was said to me, children can be so cruel to one another even at that age, the one big difference now, was, that the Davies' were most kind, and understanding, I was still disturbed over the loss of my father, but very gradually the nightmares subsided, and I was able to cope better with the situation in the room, although, I was aware that I would have to try, and get a move to another room, how I was to accomplish this I had no idea.

After retiring to bed, there was always the usual banter between us lads, serious conversation was not the order of the day, and sometimes the subject was wanking, and how many times you could come. I was totally at a loss to know what the others were talking about at first, I had had no formal tuition on sex, until that time cannot remember that I had ever been interested in the subject, I was however to know soon enough what they were about, but of course my ignorance of the facts only led to more verbal bullying. Mrs Davies must have known of my distress at being in that room, although she did not hear it from me, and I was moved to a smaller room with only six boys in total, the name of the room escapes me, all I do remember is that it was opposite the bathroom, and this helped in the morning scramble for our ablutions.

I can only remember the names of two of the boys in my room, one was Edwards, my cross country rival, and the other was Hearn. You will remember that Edwards was an accomplished footballer, and so was Hearn, but he played in goal, in fact he to had a trial for Portsmouth, but without success, I believe he played for Bognor Regis at one time.

The significance of these two boys being in this one room will now become apparent. Each winter at Arnwood. a five a side football competition was organised between the rooms, and as I said previously, I was a reasonable halfback, in other words there was very little competition from the other rooms, we had a fine goal scoring forward in Edwards when I, and the other two boys could put the ball at his feet, and Hearn would keep out most of the shots fired at him by the opposition, the only real thing we had to contend with was the pitch. A local farmer owned the field next to Arnwood, and he allowed us to set up the smaller than usual pitch, the only thing was the grass was always so long, invariably wet, and extremely uneven, however good clean fun was had by all, even though you could almost bank on us always coming out on top.

Indoor activities at Arnwood were many, and varied, everyone found something of interest, and I have no doubt that some found that they were to be grateful for the rest of their lives for the introduction at the hands of the staff, and prefects. The more physical activities such as table tennis, and billiards were the most popular, followed by board games, stamp collecting etc., one thing that most boys would have tried at some time or other would have been modelling. This took the form of Naval vessels, aircraft, and toys, these would be made for local children who had been orphaned by the war. The planes, and ships we would keep for our own amusement or to give to relatives, it was rather odd that there was as much interest in enemy aircraft as there was for the British.

Kits for a large number of ships, and aircraft were still available during this time, they consisted of part shaped balsa wood sections, a plan, and the necessary paints, I though never had the money to buy these kits, and had to borrow the plans from other boys, and find scraps of wood to construct mine.

Where did I find the wood to make my models? you may well ask, I stole it, or at least obtained it without permission, let me explain. Nearby in the town of New Milton was an aircraft factory, and they used to dump a great deal of their waste materials against a wire fence adjacent to the pavement at one point before it was collected for recycling. There were always pieces of wood, and Perspex, which I could lift quite easily by putting my arm through the wire netting. During my time at Arnwood I made numerous trips to that factory, and was never caught, I am sure that at the time I did not consider that I was doing anything wrong, but of course I was, and have no doubt that should I have been caught, I would have had to face the prospect of being expelled from school, that however did not transpire, and I had many years of modelling thanks to that factory, it may well be that they turned a blind eye, who knows.

The only tools I had at this time, was a penknife, and a small saw, this never got sharpened, and the knife used to have a new edge put on by rubbing the blade on the concrete bench top, used to work very well.

Although the tools were rather crude in their way, many fine models were produced by those of us who had the aptitude for it, my main interest was in aircraft, mainly the Spitfire, and the German counterpart the ME109, I must have made quite a few of these, but as far as I am aware none have survived. One of my models does survive somewhere I feel sure, and that was of the German pocket battleship Graff Spey, may be the spelling is incorrect, but am sure that those historians of such matters will forgive me. I was very proud of that model, and Mr.Davies suggested I might like to donate it to a local organisation, for what reason I cannot recall, I do know that it was accepted, which made me proud to think that my model would be preserved for others to enjoy in the future.

You will have gathered that the Perspex was used for the cockpits for the model planes, but it also had another use, that of making rings. As I had no drills to form the hole to take the fingure, I had to push the point of the penknife into the surface, and twist, eventually the knife would pierce the other side, and the process would begin again. Once through I would have to keep grinding away with the knife until I had a hole big enough for my finger. When this was complete the outside would be shaped, sanded, and polished with Bluebell metal polish which was still available. A long, and tedious job, but had its reward in the finished article. Why us boys should make rings, I will never know, someone must have thought up the idea, one thing was certain, it took very little in the way of materials to produce something which was quite attractive.

Many long hours were spent in those cellars making any number of things, such as tanks, train engines, dolls toys, anything in fact that could be passed on to the less fortunate of the area, and although I cannot recall any feedback from the organisations to which they were sent, I am sure that they were much appreciated.

CHAPTER 18

A More Serious Side

From the last chapter, you may have thought our life was one big round of pleasure, in most ways it was because even the more serious matters were made to be pleasurable by the staff, wrong word really, I felt them always to by my family.

One thing for sure, I lost my "loner" attitude very quickly, had to, to fit into the routine very necessary to run such a diverse bunch of children. The boys, although at school because of their academic ability, were from many differing backgrounds, rich, poor, money wise that is, we were in fact all rich being given the opportunity to study for higher education, and a better start to our working lives, this however at this time was not appreciated by most of us.

Quite apart from the normal subjects which formed the backbone of formal education, there were others which, although having a much lower profile still had a lasting influence on my life viz: music, encompassing singing, drama, and art.

Moving to Arnwood meant I once again changed choirs, this was no problem, the hostel supplied a full choir for the church in the nearby village of Hordle, once more I was singing at Matins or Evensong, sometimes both. I cannot recall how the hymns were decided upon, but I do know that often practices were taken in Mrs. Davies' sitting room around the grand piano most times with Mr. Steed as accompanist, by way of a passing comment, his very obvious sobriquet was "Cabhoss".

Most of my musical education was gained from being a member of the school orchestra, a long held tradition at the Southern. I had no preferred choice instrument, I believe I came to play the violin because of the shortage of players, I do remember attending rehearsals for some time without an instrument until my mother found me a rather battered old violin in a likewise case, of no real value, but none the less would see me through until the time that I left school.

Quite a few of the lads at Arnwood were members of the orchestra, and, like the choir, sometimes rehearsed in Mr.Davies' sitting room. I played second violin, non too well I might add, but playing at this time introduced me to classical music, something I appreciate to this day, Mrs.Davies contributed greatly to my particular love of piano pieces, she would often play for her own, and her families pleasure, and of course we would be able to hear it throughout the hostel.

I do not believe that drama was taught as a subject, although previous to the outbreak of the war, there was a tradition of performing once a year, a Gilbert, and Sullivan opera, how I would have loved to have been part of one of those productions. Although not at all sure, I think it was Arnwood that each year produced a one act play based on something familiar to most people, which in the lead up to Christmas was performed in the local village hall. I can only recall one play. The Rivals, by Sheridan, I played Mrs Malaprop, a very difficult part because the dialect is littered with "malapropisms", or misapplication of words. Many years later, I saw the complete play performed at the Chichester Festival Theatre with Patricia Routledge in the lead, she was magnificent, I could have benefited from seeing that back in the forties, although whether it would have improved my performance, who knows.

Art was something I had always enjoyed, and can remember before the war, drawing all the Disney characters, in those days only copy drawing, it was not until I attended the Southern that I learnt how to really draw, and paint with water colours. Our tutor would impart his knowledge with such enthusiasm that it made us boys enthusiastic about the results of our efforts, he was a fine water colour artist, and living in the New Forrest provided him with so many wonderful subjects to paint. I constantly look at paintings wherever I go but have never come across any of his work, perhaps he never sold any of his paintings, but only produced them for his friends to enjoy, I very much wish I had one of his works hanging on my wall, to remind me of what he taught me about the appreciation of art. It is strange that my all time favourite artist is Turner whose work was mainly in water colour, of course our tutor was not in his class, but he too loved the medium.

Some of you may wonder what happened when the weather closed in around us, as it invariably did on some winter days, sometimes for several days. There were qualified staff, and prefects at Arnwood, so we stayed put, assembled in the dining room when breakfast was cleared, and were taught in situ, usually only Maths, and English, I always had the feeling that we took in more on those days than we ever did at school. At the end of the day we had a general knowledge quiz under exam conditions, with a prize at the end, of two, and sixpence donated by R. R. I won this only once, I will never forget that day because, I was delighted to be the best on the day, but to me more importantly, I had some extra money, you never have enough of course, but to me this was a fortune, when I did receive money from home it was seldom any more than this.

CHAPTER 19

The Holidays

Under this heading I would include the weekends because they were very much holidays in that they were often spent away from Arnwood, at the allocated times, once or twice a term.

I rather think that these short breaks had to be spent at home or with a relative, I used to spend mine with my gran, ie. my mothers mother, she insisted on staying in Portsmouth throughout the war despite the air raids, it was not as though she did not have any family, she just felt that nobody was going to move her from her home, certainly not the Germans.

At this time she lived in Lake Road, a very long road which connected Commercial Road with Fratton Road, something near a mile long I would think, and she lived about halfway down in a small two up, two down terrace. When I visited her for a week end I would catch a train from Brockenhurst to Portsmouth Town Station, and walk to her house, there were trolley buses running at the time, but being a young fit individual always opted to walk. During the autumn, or winter months it was always dark when I arrived, black is a better word because there were no lights, all windows were covered with blackout material because when the air raids occurred it was very dangerous to show a light from the ground, it was strange that no one thought anything of one so young travelling alone in such conditions, I doubt that anyone in their right mind would allow it to happen in this day, and age.

I used sleep in a bedroom at the rear of the house, and would often draw the curtains back to enable me to see what was going on, particularly when the siren sounded to give warning of an impending air raid. During the latter part of the war the enemy used to send over "doodle bugs", these were small jet propelled bombs with wings, fired from ramps in France, once over the target the engine would cut out, and, and the missile, because that is what it was, would drop to the ground. I would often see these go by my window at quite a low level, that was fine, I knew we had escaped being hit, it was when you heard them coming, and the engine cutting out, and not seeing it, you could almost feel that deathly silence before the explosion as it hit the ground.

How my gran was able to feed me on my visits I will never know, she only had her own meagre rations. When I think back, I rather suspect that she went short herself for some time before my visit to make sure I had enough to eat. Sometimes I was able to take with me desert apples obtained from someone else I used to visit at other week ends, not exactly helpful to her stable diet, but she always seemed glad to have them. I daresay she shared them with her friends.

You will recall the help given to the family when my father was killed, the commanding officer at Eastney Barracks, I found out that he had a house within a few miles of Arnwood, and when he heard where I was, would invite me to tea some Sundays. I would always look forward to these occasions, the house was very grand, and the tea almost always consisted of scones with lashings of butter, jam, and cream, you can imagine how I felt with all the restriction of my normal diet at Arnwood, good though it was. Sometimes Col. Hunt would allow me to take along a friend, only one, you can imagine I would be flavour of the month when word got out of my impending next visit. It was from here that I obtained the apples when in season, I remember they were always placed in a large flat box so that they were never damaged by being on top of one another, made walking back to the hostel that bit more difficult.

The summer holidays were always spent with a family friend of my mothers, I did not know them until that first summer I spent with them, they were a lovely couple with one small child, the gentlemans name was Bob, his wife or childs name I cannot recall. Their home was a small cottage in a village in Bedfordshire, where, I have no idea, I can remember that there was no running water, just a communal well near the end of the block of terrace houses, this had to be brought up in a bucket by hand, often a frog would be an added extra! the water though was as clear as crystal, and very cold.

Bob was a farm hand, and he obtained work for me on the same farm for the whole of my summer vacation, not only was I back doing what I loved, but also getting paid for it. Unlike the farm at Faccombe, this was small, with no tractors, just horses, the harvesting done in the old fashion way, I remember that first holiday I arrived, the corn had been cut, and was in "stooks" all over the fields, dried enough, and ready to be lifted, and taken to where the rick would be built. You will remember that I enjoyed working with horses, the farm hands soon found out how good I was with them following an incident early that holiday. One of the horses was in fact an ex pit pony, very sprightly with a bit of an attitude problem, understandably really when you think it had spent so much of its life working underground. This particular morning the cart had been loaded, but before the farmhand took it back to where the rick was being built he sat on one of the shafts to drive the load back, the pony took great objection to this, and bolted, with the farmhand being thrown to the ground. I set off in hot pursuit, and did not catch up with it until it hit a barbed wire fence on the other side of the field. The poor pony was entangled, but not seriously hurt, and was very calm while I set him free, I made a fuss of him, and he was soon standing still ready to carry on, however some of the load had been shed along the way to the fence, so I led him back across the field, stopping now, and again to allow a farmhand to reload the wagon. From then on I took sole charge of that pony, and only ever led him, never sitting on the shafts, as I said previously he was rather sprightly, and it was as much as I could do to keep up with him, I became very friendly with that animal. and I am sure he appreciated the fact that I understood his needs.

I spent two summers with Bob, and his family working on that same farm, and during those happy times, although having to work hard, learnt a few skills that were new to me. There were times when "my" pony was rested, I would then be up on the cart loading the stooks being pitched up to me by a couple of farmhands. For this job you had to be very quick, not only were the stooks being fed to you quite fast, but the loading had to be done very methodically to make sure the load did not move on the way back to the rick. At other times I would be up on the rick, the same skills had to apply as with loading the cart, only more so, it would not have been appreciated had the rick been blown over during the winter. I remember one of the summers, for some reason or other, it was decided that a rick was to be threshed to obtain the grain, and a traction engine complete with a thresher duly arrived, what a sight that was with a huge belt from the engine connected to the thresher to drive all of its mechanisms. Basically the corn was fed into the top of the thresher from the rick, the straw was separated from the grain, and dragged away for future use, the grain went down a shoot into sacks, these were tied off. and changed by a farmhand, and then loaded on to a flat bed truck ready for removal to the dryer. More often than not, a baler was connected to catch the straw being discharged, I can only think that one was not available for hire at this time. I have not mentioned the task I was doing during this operation, I had the most unthankful job on earth, as you can imagine there was a great deal of noise, and dust flying about the whole area, but most of the dust created by the whole process came out under the thresher, and had to be continually cleared, this was my job. you were covered in dust the whole time, it penetrated your clothing, and made you itch like mad, not a job to be recommended.

Obviously I had other holidays throughout the year, but I cannot remember how they were spent, except on one occasion I spent it with my mother in Chilbolton, a small village near the north of Hampshire, it certainly was not xmas, probably an Easter break. Mum was housekeeper/ cook for a family known to the landowners at Faccombe, and they allowed me to stay for a while. This is another lovely part of the world, many thatched cottages, a river which at one point is quite wide complete with a fast flowing weir. I remember that there was very little to do on this break, except take in the beauty of the whole area, sometimes enough, even for someone as young as myself.

CHAPTER 20

The Return, 19ᵗʰ January 2004

S trange chapter heading, yes, but felt it necessary after not putting "pen to paper" for two years, illness, and finally a triple bi-pass operation left me with no enthusiasm for the task, however I am now quite fit, and ready to go, the only problem now is catching up with my train of thought. I have read, and re-read the last few chapters, and have decided that I will put together some unrelated facts that have come to mind over the past few weeks, and hopefully the text will start to flow.

Anyone who has lived in a boarding school situation will know, that after lights-out, sometimes all hell lets loose. The fact that the bedrooms at Arnwood were all situated around a large landing lent itself to room-raiding on a grand scale, either for "beating up" or pillow fighting, these were often a little one sided because of the number of boys in each room. You will remember I was in a small room, not such a disadvantage as you might imagine, because, if a greater number came into the room they invariably ended up falling over the beds which were so close together, we always gave good account of ourselves, and no one ever came to any harm.

You will recall that some of us had made catapults from materials "salvaged" from the aircraft factory in Christchurch, and that some of us had become quite good artists, how do I tie these together? I had at this time formed a hatred for Himler, one of Hitlers henchmen, due in part to the fact that I looked somewhat like him, round faced with metal rimmed spectacles, no moustache or cap, but when I tried an impression on one occasion, was told it was a reasonable copy of his voice, how in heavens name could anyone have known that. I had to endure some stick over this for a while, so to counteract this, I did a drawing of him, stood it on the pelmet over the window, and proceeded to catapult it, mainly with chewed paper balls, until it was shredded. This became a pass-time with a number of the lads, with sometimes the drawings depicting staff members in cartoon style.

Recently a documentary on television featured an old steam train with slam door carriages, this reminded me of an incident that happened one morning on the train to school, or more precisely as we drew into the station at Brockenhurst. Unbeknown to most of us, one of the lads from Arnwood had a carriage key, not a key in the normal sense as it was a metal "T" bar with a square shank, this turned the keep rod in the door into the jamb to lock it. We were not the only pupils travelling on the trains each day, there were a number of boys, and girls from Brockenhurst County School. On this particular day. before the last girl could alight from the carriage, the boy with the key, threw the lock. She went spare, and started to shout, to no avail, until after a while she lowered the window, and bellowed, "let I out, let I out, I can't get out oiver way". The boy with the key opened the door, and was promptly pounced on by a porter, that strange personage that no longer exists on most stations today. I cannot recall whether he was punished for what he did, one thing for sure the key was taken from him. The girl in this incident was local, and I will never forget hearing her shout those words in the vernacular.

The second year started with a new subject on the time table, Latin, the tutor's name was Rainer, yes you have guessed it, his sobriquet was "foxy", he would also be our form master for the year. Did I like Latin, no I did not, I was finding it difficult enough trying to cope with French, what I found most confusing was the way in which a sentence was laid out, ie: subject, object, and verb. Two periods a week were laid aside for this subject, one on Wednesday the other,first period the Thursday. The study was a book on the time of the Romans, the homework was always the study of a chapter set on the Wednesday, and on which we were tested on the Thursday, consistent, yes, but oh so boring.

Because Mr. Rainer was our form master, he decided that each Friday after school he would invite four or five of us at a time to his home for tea, a rota was planned, and I was among those chosen for the first outing to "foxy's" lair. We were told to meet him on the green outside the school adjacent to the road, and follow him to his home not to far away. He turned up with a massive "sit up and beg" bicycle with two seats on the cross bar, and one on the back, after a while, three young children appeared, climbed aboard. Foxy mounted, and peddled away with us following along to the rear, must have looked a bit like the Pied Piper. When we arrived at his home, we were introduced to his wife, and two more children, they were all told to take off their shoes, and socks, and to go, and milk the goats, apparently they only ever drank goats milk. This was a bit of a culture shock even to us, but I remember we were treated most kindly, and the rules of the house were not imposed on us. I cannot remember what we had for tea that afternoon, it certainly was nothing cooked, so we missed out on high tea that day!

When I look back, boys, and probably girls can be very cruel to staff who are kindly, but susceptible to the odd joke, but this I think was particularly bad, and I was party to it. Mr. Tilney our French master, agreed at our suggestion, to chair a debate on religion, we knew that he was a true Christian, and made out that we would like to know more about his faith. These sessions, there were more than one, were rather like the lamb to the slaughter, I attended a couple, and then dropped out because I was so ashamed of what I was being party to, fortunately, I do not think that Mr.Tilney knew what was going on, no harm done, but a stark lesson for me, and one I have never forgotten.

Brockenhurst stands on the river Test, not exactly large or fast flowing but in those days teeming with fish, and other wildlife, I used to spend many hours "fishing" although you could hardly call it that because all I had was a length of string tied to a branch of a tree with a bent pin for a hook, yes I really did use a bent pin. Bait was either bread or worms, neither seemed to work too well as I can recall I only ever had one catch, a small tiddler, and that was thrown back for the kingfishers.

Seeing a Kingfisher these days is rather rare except on television, but in those days the sight of this beautiful bird as it immerged from a hole in the bank. settle on a tree branch overhanging the river, and then dive for fish was something I will never forget. These days I only see this on television, but still wonder at the way it catches its food, a never ending task when it has young to feed.

Invariably when young people are thrown together as we were at Arnwood, secret societies are formed, we were no exception, one stands out because there is usually one thing uppermost in the minds of the young, food with a capital "F".

I had formed a very close relationship with two lads in my year, both living in my hostel, Roger Watts, and Bert White, I did not know it at the time, but we would remain close friends until the onset of our National Service, when we became of age, twenty one years. Roger was quite a plump lad who certainly loved his food more than Bert, or I, so I think it was probably his idea to start the Blamuel Society with the prime idea of obtaining more food than our rations allowed, mainly through parcels from home, or whatever, and sharing it out among the members, and usually being devoured in places away from the rest of the lads. We had a motto, in Latin no less which I will try, and remember, I hope there are no classical scholars reading this because I think I will be in all sorts of trouble, Omnes Grubbabus Comitabus Blamuelorum, which loosely translated means. All good grub comes from Blamuel. Great fun at the time, but like all such societies, did not last very long.

Roger, Bert, and I had one all consuming interest, cycling, none of us had bikes, but Roger had regular copies of cycling magazines sent from home which we would all read from cover to cover. Our aim was to eventually have racing cycles, and to compete on both the road, and the track, this we accomplished after the war with a certain amount of success, particularly as juniors up to the age of eighteen years. Strange that such an interest could develop without the main ingredient, ie. a bike, however it did, and not to the detriment of our school work.

Following lunch each day at school, providing the weather was okay, most of us would go to the field area where two games were played out on a regular basis, one gentle, the other quite violent.

In the days before decimal coins became the norm, among the copper coinage were farthings, halfpennies, and pennies, these were used to throw against a wall, dropped to the ground, and the idea was that the next coin thrown would fall and cover the previous coin thrown, should this happen you won the coin covered. I have no idea of the precise rules of the game because I never had enough money to indulge myself, but would admit to watching with a great deal of interest, some of the boys were probably the gamblers of the future.

The game I was very much involved with, had to have two players as a team, one riding on the others back. The idea was to get as many pairs as possible lined up along one edge of the field, each pair would be allocated a number, and one pair would be nominated to stand out in front about twenty yards from the line. The pair in front would shout a number, and the idea was for that pair to run, and try to make it to the other side without being brought down, if they made it every one would charge across the open ground, with pair in the middle trying to bring down as many as they could, should they not make it, another number was shouted, and the process would start again. Eventually it was hoped that all bar one pair would be in the middle, and an almighty fight ensued for the last pair to try, and make it through the horde! The odds of surviving to the last were remote, I used to often have a good run because I was small, and light, and invariably on the back of one of the larger boys, a tough old game, but I cannot recall any serious injuries.

There was a pastime which was both fun, educational, and sometimes quite challenging in that it developed ones communication skills. I believe this was carried out during the days when the inclement weather kept us at Arnwood, although I cannot be sure of that. A number of subjects were written on pieces of paper, and put into a container, one of you were asked to pick a subject at random, and stand in front of the gathering, and speak for three minutes, quite difficult if you know nothing about the subject chosen, but of course the idea is that even if you know nothing, you spout a load of rubbish, and hope you can make it convincing, I remember I had to speak once on the Penny Black stamp, not too difficult at that time because I had a passing interest in stamp collecting.

CHAPTER 21

The Beginning of the End

From what I have so far written, you could be forgiven for thinking that the war had gone by us without a thought for what was happening around the world, this was not so, for me personally, I had more than enough reason for never ever forgetting this period in my life. We were in fact kept up to date with all that went on, mainly through the radio, and the newspapers, but also through conversations with the staff both at school, and Arnwood.

The whole war came into sharp focus in the months prior to the allied landings in France, all around Brockenhurst were forests as well as heathlands, and I used to walk these areas quite regularly, that is, until the whole area was invaded by the Canadian army. We were not aware of it at the time, but the preparations were under way for the invasion of Europe with embarkation from Lymington, and Southampton. The sight as you walked through the forest was unbelievable, there were tanks, armoured vehicles, lorries, jeeps, armoury of every description, and thousands of men. I recall that the men were extending the exhausts to all the vehicles to terminate above the height of the vehicles, and covering everything with a grease like substance, it was very obvious that all the vehicles would have to engage the sea before reaching the beaches. There did not appear to be much restriction on our movements among these troops, they were always pleased to see us, and, they were very generous with their chocolate rations, we very rarely saw sweets of any sort, so you can imagine how we felt about having these wonderful treats.

I do not think that any of us placed much store on the fact that we were surrounded by Canadian troops, they were fun to associate with, and, there was the small matter of the hand outs, but no sooner had we got accustomed to their presence in the area, a walk one day found that they had gone. Not a trace told us that anybody had been in the area, not only had they gone, but the whole area had been cleaned, only one give away, tyre, and track marks, these, though always in abundance from the tractors belonging to the farmers, were more in evidence, and deeper.

I am sure that at this time we were not fully aware that this really was the "beginning of the end" of the war. Life went on as it had always done, and when the invasion of Europe did commence there were many setbacks, with the end to the conflict seeming a long way off. We were made aware of what was going on, and gradually most of the boys were looking forward to going back to Portsmouth, for me, things were by no means certain, our old house was rented, we had no idea whether it was still standing, and the store which housed our furniture may well have been bombed. When the war in Europe did come to an end, I heard from mother that she had found a place for us to live, not our old house, because although it survived the war, somebody else now lived there.

Try as I may I have no recollection of the move back to Portsmouth, obviously we were informed when. and where the school would operate from, you will remember the old building was bombed, I cannot even remember saying my goodbyes to the staff at the hostel, it may well have been that I knew I would almost certainly meet up with those who had grown close to me ie. Mrs. Davies, and her two children, Mary, and Gwyneth, as it happens, apart from R. R. I was only to see them for a few times, and when they eventually retired, and moved to Cornwall I lost track of them completely until recently finding out that both Mr. & Mrs. Davies had passed on, but their children were well, with families if their own. Gwynneth I have seen again, but not as yet Mary, Gwynneth is small, and tiny of build just like my own dear wife.

The school we were to occupy for the rest of my time at the Southern, was Albert Road. It was situated next to the Odeon cinema between Festing Road, and St. Ronans Road, very old with very few facilities. There was a play ground facing on to the main road, a hall, no laboratory, and sufficient classrooms to accommodate our numbers, you can imagine, our education was going to fall short of the required standard for a while until a new promised school was built on the Eastern Road, Baffins Road junction, I know a school was built there, whether it was for the Southern I have no idea. I only know that my formal education was completed at the Albert Road premises.

So began my final year, a fact I was not to know until later, my intention was to get into the six form, and hopefully go on to university, I had formed this idea in my head that I could teach, something born out a number of years later when I had a great deal of success teaching apprentices the skills in being a Joiner, and Cabinet Maker.

CHAPTER 22

A Different World

The house mother had found for us to live in, on a rented basis, was in Clive Road, Frattton, in Portsmouth, at the junction with Adames Road. The corner property was a shop converted into a gents hairdressers, only one operative, the owner of the whole property, a very pleasant man who had apparently invested his gratuity in the business when he left the army.

Once again the family were united, well, not quite, my mother, brother Douglas, and my two sisters. Daphne, and Sheila, my other two brothers, Edward, and Dennis were still away at Naval School, myself of course, and my cousin Rob, how he came to be living with us I have no idea, I only know that I very much regretted the fact because of what was to happen later.

From Clive Road I would walk to school each day, quite a way, but it was not as far as the walk from Arnwood to the station at Sway. As far as I can remember there were no kitchens at the new school so a packed lunch was the order of the day, probably bread, and jam, I say that, because when I eventually went to work, that was what mother used to pack for me, a standing joke among my workmates because I had no love for it, thankfully the Seagulls were not so fussy, and only too pleased to scoff the left overs, and sometimes the lot.

My pal Roger lived in Lorne Road, Southsea, well within walking distance of school, but my other pal Bert lived in Laburnum Grove, North End, and can only assume that he came to school by bus, no mothers with cars in those days, however we all managed okay until we were able to purchase our first bikes, more of that later.

Before returning to school after the summer holidays, discussions took place as to what course I would pursue in my final year. At this time I was in the "B" class, I dropped from the "A" after my second year, and rather expected to take my School Certificate, rather like GCSE's of today, except that you had to pass all ten subjects to be awarded the certificate, however the headmaster moved the goalposts that term, and , in an effort to encourage more boys into the six form, ruled that only boys in the "A" class could take it, boys like myself would have to stay at school for a further year to take it, and so be a year late starting in the six form, I would have probably accepted that, but my mother dropped a bombshell in telling me that I must go to work when I had completed my four years at the Southern, apparently, so she said, her widows pension allowance for me would stop when I reached sixteen, something I always felt would not have happened should I have been allowed to stop on.

As far as the school was concerned, there were very few options open to you on completion of the normal span, six form, the civil service, the dockyard, or leaving, taking the dockyard entrance exam was very much frowned upon, but just about accepted, and I opted to go down this route, taking the view that it was better to obtain a trade than taking my chance at finding a job I may never be satisfied with. I made my choice clear at school, and they arranged for me to sit the exam the following spring.

I do not know who made the case for street parties all over Britain, but it was accepted with much enthusiasm, committees were formed to organise the "bun fights", and entertainment, little did I know at the time that I would be an intrinsic part of that entertainment. You will remember that my cousin lived with us, he had a wonderful 120 bass piano accordian, which he allowed me to play, something I had never done before, but, having a sound knowledge of music I soon learnt to play by ear, someone organising the party must have heard of my somewhat dodgy prowess, and asked me to play at the party. What I did, was, learnt half a dozen or so of tunes popular at the time, and hoped that I would be able to entertain the children, and parents by having breaks, and playing the songs in different order each time. Our street party like all the others around Portsmouth during that late summer of 1945 was a resounding success. All streets were closed to traffic, trestle tables were set up down the centre of the road, with chairs each side supplied by the residents, quite a number were those were from front rooms, they rarely saw the light of day, let alone anyone sitting on them, but this was something special, the end of the war, with much to celebrate for most people, I say that, because of course my dad was never coming back, and a lot of the dads were not available for the parties because they were still in their operational areas.

Where all the food came from I will never know, but the tables were laden with all the goodies associated with parties at that time ie: bread, and margerine, jellies, and cakes, a wonderful time was had by all, I played the accordian, and ended the proceedings walking up, and down the street with the children, and parents following me, and singing at the top of their voices. That memory will always be with me, not only because the day went so well, but of the sadness, knowing that my dear dad could not be part of the proceedings, I know that he would have wanted us, his family, to be part of that happiness, perhaps he was looking down on us with an approving grin, I hope so.

Coming back to Portsmouth seemed to alter my perception of the church, I was not aware of it at the time, but events to follow, will give you an idea of what I mean. Since I now lived in Clive Road it seemed good sense to contact the vicar at St. Mary's church just a stones throw away, this I did, whether it was my age, my voice had broken, or that I was not known in the district, I do not know, but he made a good case for me not being part of the choir, and suggested I join the youth section which had their own meeting, and service each Sunday afternoon, this I did. I must admit to quite enjoying those Sunday afternoons, it did not interfere with any of my other activities, and it was much more grown up. We had discussions not only on religious matters, but on everyday problems we needed to talk about, and a service at which we were, on a regular basis expected to read the lesson.

Across the road from the church was the Building School, and, having areas that could be rented, the church decided that it would open a youth club for those of us who attended the Sunday afternoon youth section, and to be run entirely by the members. A committee was set up to lay the ground rules, and organise the activities to include a snack bar, I did not get involved in this because of my other interests, and my school work, very necessary because of my impending exam, I did however volunteer to collect the crisps for the snack bar each week.

I rather think, that at this time there was only one company in England producing crisps, that being Smith's, and their factory was in Mile End, you did not need instructions how to get there, you could smell the cooking fat a mile away. In those days the packets had small sachets of salt inside allowing you the option of having salt or not, oddly enough this idea is catching on again, what goes around comes around, I seem to recall that twelve packets were packed in square tins, each packet was a good deal larger than they are today. Usually I would have to collect either two or four tins, I would have to pay cash, and the tins would be tied together so that I could carry them in each hand. Collecting these goods was an education, the factory was manned completely by women, and often when I approached the doors there would be a number of them standing having a smoke, they would be wearing cooking oil soaked overalls, hats, and often clogs on their feet, generally not looking too wholesome. You can imagine the remarks I had thrown at me, not just the language, but sexual, and not innuendo, I hate to think what would have happened had I stopped, and encouraged them, but at that time I was all very innocent!

The youth section of St. Mary's church was proving to be a great success, only one thing was lacking, and that was numbers. Youth clubs generally were to become popular, but when associated with the church it was difficult to command attention from young people, they always imagined that religion was going to be rammed down their throats, and with some justification. At one of our regular meetings with the vicar, I suggested that we invite youngsters off the street to join our club. and so increase the numbers that way, the vicar was quite vehement, pointing out that he only wanted people who were willing to attend his church. Normally I was very placid, but in this instance I felt very strongly that this was the wrong message to be sending out by a so called Christian man, and I told him so. My questioning him only made matters worse, and he would not budge from his argument, the upshot of this encounter was, that I left the church, never to go back. From then on I only attended church on special occasions, although, the one thing I did not lose, was my faith, I often say to people that you do not have to attend church to be a Christian, acts always speak louder than words, I will now come down from my soapbox!

CHAPTER 23

Changes

Before going on to changes in my life at this time, I must tell you of something which happened while I was still at Brockenhurst. Discipline was very strict at school, and corporal punishment was still allowed, although only administered when a breach of discipline was such that an outside factor came into play. Only once did I see this enacted, and it quite traumatised me, partly due to fear, the absolute wrong reason to keeping order, especially among young people. In this instance, three boys had broken into a service establishment, to steal goods which they were to sell on, they were caught by the police, who, in their wisdom, decided that the head should deal with the matter. Mr. Jones obviously interviewed the boys, and then one morning at assembly, which he decided to take, the boys were led in, and stood in front of the whole school. The head relayed their escapade to us all, and proceeded to outline the punishment to be handed down, they were to receive six strokes of the cane, and expelled from school. The lads concerned were in their final year, and from the lower end of the forth year, whether they were humiliated I will never know. but it was certainly a lesson for the rest of us. They were, one at a time told to stand on a sheet of A4, bend over, and the six strokes given with what seemed to be all the force the head could muster, they were then dismissed, and never seen again, you can imagine we were all very subdued when we trooped off to our first period of the day.

Coming back to school in Portsmouth was an all new ball game, it was rather like operating from a box after the freedom of the countryside, of course I wanted the war to finish as soon as possible just like every other sane citizen, but I had it fixed in my mind that I would complete my schooling at Brockenhurst. The periods carried on much as before except for the practical elements of chemistry, and science due to lack of laboratories, sport training I believe was carried out on a sports field at Baffins where the new school was to be built. This I do not remember, but training must have been carried out because in the following spring, early summer inter schools sports championships were revived, and were to take place at the Royal Naval sports arena at Pitt Street.

Although my main sport interest was cycling, school dictated that I pursue other events, and because cross country was no longer an option, I trained for the mile [now the 1500 mtrs.], and the high jump, the two were hardly compatible, but I somehow qualified to represent the school in my age group for both events. The afternoon was very enjoyable, except for my dismal performance in both events, although I came close to the school high jump record, I failed to get a place in either event, I felt I had let myself down, and more to the point, the Southern, this was the only opportunity I had of representing the school, and I had blown it big time. There was one significant victory that afternoon in the cricket ball throwing event, that was won by Tony Aspinall, I remember this because Tony was a member of my house, the blues, so in the inter house events I often competed along side of him, he was a couple of years ahead of me, very tall, and of large build, and a natural in his chosen sport. Whilst at school I had no knowledge of Tony's family, but years later I met up with him at a business function, and there was instant recognition on both sides, and as you can imagine we had plenty to talk about. His father ran a very large haulage contractors, and when he passed away, Tony took over the reins, during the years I was in business we often met up, but rarely did we talk of our school days, I suppose for him his life was pre-destined, and that school was just a necessary evil.

Home life was not happy, I resented my cousin living with us for a number of reasons, the main one being his self election as head of the family, and his conduct whenever any of us came into conflict with him,

I think I was the only one he used to hit, thankfully, because he was about six feet four, and very big with it so could inflict a lot of damage. I did not understand why he was living with us from the start, but it soon came to light that it was mother, apparently a physical attraction despite the age gap, I had no idea of the legal implication of this union. I only know that it made me feel sick, this feeling stayed with me until I left home to get married. I still suffered periodic nightmares about dad, although no one knew of that, these days of course you could obtain help with such matters, but in those days you were expected "to pull yourself together".

One significant change occurred while a member of St Mary's youth section ie: an awareness of the opposite sex, a little late compared to today, I was coming up to fifteen years old. A girl joined the church, I rather think because of the club activities, although I cannot be sure of that, all I do know, is that all the male members thought she was stunning. The film stars of the day were invariably statuesque, with hour glass figures, and long lustrous hair, that was Kathy, and although I must admit to taking notice of her, that was as far as it went, other lads tried to "date" her, but with no luck. it was not as though she was averse to the opposite sex, but her father would not have approved, he was a right bruiser, and we were all afraid of him, perhaps he was quite a gentle man, one thing for certain, we were not taking any chances. It was another year or so before I had my first girlfriend, nothing very serious on my part, not so on hers though, and that was the end of that, and although I formed a platonic association with another girl, she was only a stop gap until my future wife Mary came along when I was eighteen, and then we did not married until I was twenty one, and we were still virgins!, that is another story.

Some changes may seem insignificant, for instance the food that mum served up, at Arnwood I was used to having very regular meals, and they included two cooked, now, although what she put up was okay, it was as though it was all a bit of a chore, strange, when during the war she cooked for the gentry with dishes prepared for all occasions, it always surprised me that she did not vary our diet too much, perhaps money was tight, I would have thought not, because all our family allowances then would have been supplemented by Rob being at work, and I believe he had a pension from the army following a quite horrific motor cycle accident, however I of course got used to it, a matter of having to, I had no means of altering the fact.

You will recall my saying that we had no laboratory facilities at Albert Road, well, I had from my chemistry lessons loved making crystals, and in particular, copper sulphate, and sulphur, so decided to have my own laboratory at home, with disastrous consequences. At the rear of the house was a scullery come kitchen, and this particular Saturday afternoon I was turning a copper sulphate crystal that I had growing in a glass, it was I remember beginning to look like a Saphire, as it should, but I also decided to attempt to form a sulphur crystal, any of you out there who knows what this element smells like when it is burning will know the consequences of my action, horrendous, I was nearly choking, and the whole house smelt terrible, as you can imagine I was in real trouble, one of the times I was "punished" by Rob, and told never to attempt the process again.

Although our home was by no means spacious we did seem to manage, that is until we had two additions to the household, they were my gran, and grandad, on my fathers side, I have no idea why they came to stay with us, I can only assume that they were made suddenly homeless, and mum took them in. Both were well into their seventies, but at the time appeared to be quite fit, gran was tall, and elegant, not in the way that she dressed, but the way she carried herself, a very kind, and gentle person, grandad was shorter, bald, and never smiled. They had fourteen children, so gran, had until they grew up, had a very hard life, grandad was rarely at home until he retired, he was a merchant seaman, sailing the world in large sailing ships, and whilst away would always build models of the ship he was serving on at the time, I must say that they were excellent, particularly when you take into account he had no plans, and very few tools, most of the family seemed to have one of these models mounted in a glass case, and on display in their front rooms. I had had no contact with my grandparents for a number of years, so had no idea what they were really like, having them live with us was a bit of a culture shock, particularly as grandfather was so awful to gran, he had no respect for her, and would shout at her for the slightest thing whether it was something she said or did, although having no proof of this, I always felt that in the past he would beat her.

As I have said, gran was a lovely person, and would often cook for us, an improvement over the normal fare that mum prepared, but although she would do this for us, they always chose to eat in their own room. They had, what I can only describe as a bedsit, quite a large room situated on the ground floor at the rear of the barbers shop, I always thought it was dark- and dismal, confirmed, to me at least, when something else happened a little later.

My grandparents stay was to be very short, after only a few months gran became ill, and died, and as was the custom in those days, she lay in her bed with nightlights burning until the day of her burial, these lights were changed as, and when by Rob, I am glad to say, although I did go to her room to see her, only the once, you can imagine what that room was like with the curtains drawn, and just a nightlight burning, and the smell of death, not something you forget as a young person. Grandad did not take the loss of his wife at all well, he cried a great deal, and was often found slumped over her body, I think his past attitude to this wonderful old lady was coming back to haunt him. Following the funeral, he stayed with us for only a short while, he became impossible, and mum could not cope, fortunately, one of his daughters lived quite close, she ran a public house just inside Arundel Street, and agreed to take him in, she supplied him with tobacco, and all the drink he required, and, although he seemed happy enough, he only lasted a few months, and without becoming ill, died, of what I do not know, but I daresay the loss of his dear wife played some part in it.

CHAPTER 24

Cycling, The Passion

Had it not been for the fact that I had to leave school the following year, I believe my interest in cycling would have seriously affected my studies, as it was, I had to concentrate on the Dockyard entrance exam, at the time I remember I did not consider that a problem.

My first priority was to obtain a bike, difficult when there was so little money, that is pocket money, but Roger's brother came to the rescue. He knew someone who had been released from the R.A.F. who had set up a business re-spraying cars, and suggested to him that he could carry out the same service on bike frames, with our contacts in the local cycling clubs we found him the clients, and he employed Roger, Bert, and myself to clean the old paint off the frames, and prepare them for spraying. I recall that this was quite hard work, especially when the frame was finished in black stove enamel, however, needs must, and we always seemed to have plenty of work, and at ten shillings a time, the savings soon grew to a tidy sum.

Although I had no bike, Roger, and Bert did, so we joined the North End Cycling Club, I cannot remember what bike Roger had, but Bert had found his dream machine, a Helyett, considered at that time as one of the best of French road machines, and, there was only one other like it in the Portsmouth area, and that belonged to Tony Hempell, also in our club. With everyone on the look out for something for me, I soon heard of a frame for sale in Gosport. we took the ferry across the harbour, located the address, and found that it was a Sun, would not have been my first choice, but it was a well known British machine that had the potential to be built into a first time bike even for competition work, the cost was three pounds, just in budget.

There were a lot of more senior club members who had spare parts left over from before the war, and with their help I soon had my bike up, and running, some spares were even given to me free, but not all. Where I had to buy new parts, I went to Bill Harvel's shop in Hilsea, he was most helpful, and the three of us spent many hours on a Saturday afternoon talking shop with him. For those of you not familiar with the name. Bill was a member of the British Olympic four man team pursuit squad that won a medal at the 1932 games in Los Angeles, America, a modest man who would only talk of that time if pressed, his medal was thrown in a drawer in the workshop at the rear of his shop, I believe he was probably proud of his achievement, but he certainly did not speak of it much.

It was some time before the cycling track at Alexander Park was re-opened, because although it had not been damaged by bombing, there had been anti-aircraft guns mounted around the track, and they caused quite a bit of damage. The local authority did give some priority to the matter, and eventually it was re-opened, not one of the best of tracks, it being too big, a third of a mile round instead of the normal quarter of a mile, because it had to accommodate the running track inside, it did not matter to any of us at the time, it was back in action, and we could look forward to the local track league clubs competing with one another again.

From this time until I was called up for National Service in late 1951 my cycling was a serious pursuit, with training most days, on the road, and the track, quite difficult because of the amount of homework heaped upon us most evenings during the run up to the dockyard exam. Once I began to realise some potential as a junior rider the priority was a better machine, the Sun was much too heavy, and the design not the best, certainly not for track work. My next bike was a Bates, more a track bike than road, it had very distinctive diadrant forks, only produced by this company, these had the affect of reducing the wheel base, but making it a very firm ride, okay for the track, but not conducive to long rides on the road.

This bike served me well until after I left school in fact, when I eventually had a road, and track machine, but that is another story. My time cycling whilst at school, and up to my call up for National Service was wonderful, the close companionship of my two pals, and competition success particularly as a junior, memories never to forget. I recall that in club events where medals were awarded, the officials would allow us younger members to take the equivalent value of the medal in vouchers for the local cycle shops, I have no medals to show for my successes because that is what I used to do! I have however reports showing some of what I achieved, at the time buying a new saddle or whatever was much more important than medals, sometimes I do wish that I had been able to accept the award in the form of a medal, if only to pass on.

Time trialing on the road was traditionally carried out on country roads in the early hours of Sunday morning, and the dress of the day had to be black, something we thought was ridiculous, we would often turn up "out of dress" much to the consternation of the officials, particularly the local time keeper, Albert Earwacker who was getting on a bit even then. At this time a National break away had been formed. The British League of Racing Cyclists, who used to massed start race on the open roads in bright coloured gear, just as they did in races like the Tour de France. You can imagine, this was how we wanted to dress, and gradually that is what we did, a quiet revolution. The League did encounter very serious problems at times, because it was illegal to race on the roads in this manner, and attempts at sabotage were common, however, eventually all opposition was overcome, and Britain followed Europe, the first step towards the EU perhaps? One event was allowed, the Brighton to Glasgow stage race, the forerunner of the Round Britain much later, the three of us regularly went to Brighton to see the start on the sea front, how we looked forward to that, mingling with the riders while they prepared their bikes, quite a few would be famous riders of the day from the continent,

I have black, and white photos of the event from one year, not that I need them, the memories are as vivid today as they were then, the massed start of all the riders in their bright gear was something to behold on a wonderful summers day.

The popularity of massed start racing prompted the ruling body of the time to think of alternative ways of racing other than on the roads, and came up with the idea of circuit racing. There were plenty of un-used air-bases around the country, and, following minor repairs to the perimeter roads were soon in use at weekends. The only one close to Portsmouth with a perimeter road was on the Goodwood Estate, near Chichester, this was privately owned, but no objections were put forward to the local clubs using it provided that the required dates did not clash with the motor sport events. The circuit was in excess of four miles so was ideal for the purpose, only one problem was encountered when the cycling event followed the day after the cars, and that was oil spillage, quite dangerous if a patch could not be avoided, I cannot recall any serious accidents, and this venue was used until the owners decided to up grade the whole circuit complete with a grandstand, and to use it only for motor sports, over the years all the most famous drivers from around the world have appeared here, now though it is only used for special events, the demands of modern F1 racing could not be met on this circuit without massive investment.

I will only recount one event, and I rather think it was the first following the re-opening of Goodwood, not a large field that day because the tradition of time trialing was still dominant, I have a feeling that the three of us, Roger, Bert. and myself may well have been the only riders from the Northenders, we decided to turn out as a team, and because the club had no special colours to race in, we purchased red "T" shirts to go with our black skin tight shorts, white socks, and white caps, smaller than the modem base ball caps, and as worn by all the continental riders, to complete the ensemble, Bert's mother embroidered across the back of the shirts in very large letters, PNECC the club initials, we were the only team turned out in this manner, we at least looked the part, but it was not to the liking if the club officials, they did not appreciate that we were trying to move the club into the twentieth century, we were just young upstarts bucking the system, what's new.

In the longer distance events, such as these massed start ones, we carried aluminium feeding bottles in a cage fixed to the down tube of our bikes, and mine was always filled with glucose water. Before the start of the above event, I cannot remember which of my two mates it was, but one of them produced some large round tablets which he said were supplements mainly of glucose, but what else, who knows, we were all persuaded to chew some before the race started following assurances that they were harmless. About five miles into the race we were dropped by a break away group along the back straight, suddenly, disaster struck, I collapsed falling painfully to the ground, my two pals stopped to help me, but I did not appear to be hurt to badly. The whole episode was seen from the other side of the track, and help was soon to hand, apart from graizing, I was breathless, and distressed, but nothing untoward was found wrong with me, however, although saying nothing about the tablets we had taken to anybody, the three of us were worried that something more sinister may be wrong. That was the last supplement we ever took, and I only relate what happened all those years ago because of what is going on today, what goes around, comes around.

CHAPTER 25

The Final Year

During my final year at the Southern, although I had to concentrate much more on my academic studies, this in no way diminished my enthusiasm for cycling. My two pals, and myself even took on the persona of our favourite international cyclist, mine was Bartali, a top Italian road man who had great success in all the major races around Europe, I was often told that I looked somewhat like him, slim with a prominent Roman nose, sometimes it was said rather insultingly, but I always took it as a compliment.

The training continued, I competed in junior events on the road, and the track, and when not competing watched others performing, and not just at Alexander Park, regular visits were made to the Southampton track, and occasionally to Herne Hill in London, always something special because we would only go there when a top international meeting was planned. I remember on one occasion, the three of us plus another lad called John Lattrizza cycled to Heme Hill to a meeting specifically to see one person, Scheerans, the spelling may be wrong, but I know he was Belgium, and the world sprint champion of the day. One thing stands out in the memory of him, and that was when he came out on the track to warm up he was wearing thick brown woollen tights, now I understand that sprinters have to keep their muscles warm, but this was a very hot summers day, and I would have thought that was taking things a bit too far.

We saw some wonderful racing that afternoon, and eventually set off for home in the early evening, all four of us were rather exhausted from sitting in the hot sunshine, and leaping up, and down cheering on our favoured riders. All went well until we were riding up the Petersfield side of Butser Hill, when John said that he could no longer go on, we tried to encourage him to continue, even to the extent of trying to push him, but to no avail, I do not think that he had ever ridden more than thirty miles before, in cycling parlance, he had the "bonk". John decided he would bed down for the night in the bracken of a nearby wood, so we left him, and continued on our way home, at the time we thought nothing of it, but his mother must have wondered where he was, or did she, we had no way of knowing, we do know that the following day he turned up as bright as a button.

I would like to relate one item of interest with regard to cycling before going on to the rest of the year. Quite late that summer of 1945, I was in a position to consider buying a true road machine, and to that end took to reading the "for sale" sections in the cycling magazines., I did not have the where withal to purchase a new one, it had to be second hand, I eventually found what I was looking for, and phoned the London number, the gentleman who answered seemed very educated, and offered to bring the cycle to Portsmouth the following Sunday, it was a France Sport, another well know French machine.

Sure enough, on the Sunday afternoon a Military jeep drew up outside our house, I remember it had an enclosed back, so I could not see what he had brought, I opened the door, and he introduced himself, and his wife who had come with him for the ride, he told me the France Sport was his wifes machine, and that he had brought his own bike as well for me to look at, apparently they used them for recreation around Hyde Park, but having now been posted, he was an army captain, would not require the bikes. Imagine my surprise when he opened up the back of the jeep, and saw his bike, a Helyett, identical to my pal Bert's, you can imagine, I drooled over it, but could not consider buying it because of the price, we did however strike a deal on the Sport, and I paid him fourteen pounds, it was in immaculate condition, metallic blue, with all aluminium accessories ie: wheels, cranks, handlebars, brakes, gears etc. I really could not believe my good fortune at such a bargain, it served me well with just minor changes, until in fact I got married, a priority, I was very reluctant to see it go.

During spring of 1946 I sat the dockyard exam, I had thought that I would be taking the School Certificate, so found that by comparison, it was much easier by virtue of the number of subjects required to be taken, I am not sure, but I think they were. Maths, English, and General Knowledge, and took just one day to complete. As far as I was concerned, that was it, from then on, although I would have liked to carry on studying with my usual enthusiasm, I had nothing left to give, I felt that my whole life had been taken from me by depriving me of the opportunity to go forward to teaching, quite wrong as it happens, doors always open for you, just take the chance when something presents itself to you, a lesson soon learnt when I eventually commenced in the work place.

Although the war in Europe had been over for a year or so, plans were under way for the construction of a huge council estate on the slopes of Portsdown Hill, at Paulsgrove. Mother put the family name forward for accommodation on this estate because where we were living in Clive Road was only temporary, I had no way of knowing then, but I would live there until I got married, and mother lived there for many years.

My pals, and I were not unlike the young of today, in that we often did not agree with those in authority, with us it was mainly the elderly members of the cycling club, some were well beyond their sell by date, and had no intention of dragging themselves into the next century, on the whole we did not want very much, just to dress differently, and be listened to occasionally, not much to ask for you may think, so what has changed, not much. As I said previously, the BLRC, quite impressed us, however, we had no intention of joining them because they were very limited in what they could do at that time, but what we could do, was form our own club, affiliate ourselves to the National Ass., and compete against all the other clubs in the district, to this end we planned how we would go about it to make the biggest impact, this came to fruition, but not until after I had left the Southern.

You may have thought from reading the above, that we did not get on too well with members of the North End Club, quite the contrary, most of them were more than helpful to us, and liked the success we had in competition with other clubs, but this was one of the oldest cycling clubs in the country, but really needed an injection of younger blood in their administration, we knew that this was not going to happen, and that is what prompted us to take the action that we did. One member did stand out as a good friend, he was Jack Smith, he served in the army during the conflict, and returned to his old club unscathed, to take up his position as the number one sprinter of the day. He was a gentle giant, very white, never getting a suntan, and always willing to help anybody, I recall he did not reign too long as the number one sprinter, as always, someone younger comes along, and de-thrones you, this did not bother Jack, he converted an old motor cycle into a pace making machine, and introduced pace events to Portsmouth. Jack was one of life's rare people, he was eventually recognised by the city, and went on to be the youth coach for the Portsmouth area, I am proud to have known him, unfortunately he died quite young, I hope, like me, many people still remember him.

That summer was enjoyed so much by us three pals, "the muscateers", inseparable, in the knowledge that it was to be the last spent with so much freedom. Although we were still taking our cycling very seriously, our approach was distinctly nonchalant, we all knew that this time was to be savoured because it was never going to happen again. So much was about to change, new friends would be made, the work ethic with all it's facets had to be taken on board, so much less time to ourselves, there was so much that we were looking forward to, albeit with some trepidation, on the other hand there would be challenges, and I for one was looking forward to those, my inbred competitive spirit was always there for me, something I never lost all the time I was at work, or for that matter at play.

A month or so before the end of term, I heard that I had passed the Dockyard entrance exam, and was given a date to attend the dockyard for the selection of a job, I had very little idea what I wanted to do in truth, I know I rather fancied being an electrician, but that was not to be. Mother came with me on the day, not to influence me in the choice of job, but rather, I suspect to ensure that I took something to get me on the "wage" ladder. When we arrived there were several hundred boys gathered, an indication of the apprenticeships on offer in those days, there was a very large chalk board with all the jobs listed, and the numbers of each trade required, quite a number of electrical fitters, I remember there were two pattern makers, and two MCD joiners, and so on, and, according to where you were placed in the exam, that determined your choice. Surprisingly, I thought I was high enough on the list, to get the choice I wanted, but not so, and ended up choosing the MCD joiner, and cabinet maker, as it happens, a fine choice, and one I never ever regretted.

During July of that year, I left the Southern, I had said my goodbyes to those few masters I felt had been especially kind to me over the years, in particular Mr. R. R. Davies, he had been a father figure for so long, and I owed him a huge debt of gratitude, "Shacks" Shackleton of course, and "Tish" Tilney, rather sad when you think of the number of staff who contributed to my education during those, what I now realise, were very informative years. Had I gone into the six form I have no doubt that I would have had a totally different outlook when I left, but that was not to be, what I did not know when I left, was that my education was to continue at The Dockyard Technical College for a further three years to Lower National Standard, that section of my education was to be the very corner stone of everything I achieved in the future, although at the time I was not to be aware of that.

Now that I knew what I was going to do as a job, you notice I have not said career, I, and my friends were going to make the most of our summer holiday, when you are young you never really appreciate those long breaks, and often, best use was not made of them. The job I had chosen was a natural progression from the days when I was interested in model making, it never entered my head that I would be doing it for a living, that however would be at the end of a five year apprenticeship, now the summer was calling. I did hear during this recess of my commencement date, 29.10.46, and was told to report to the MCD joiners shop at a given time to be allocated an instructor, he would in normal circumstances have seen me through to the end of my five years, but in this case, that was not to be because my allocated gentleman decided to take a post with the dockyard in Simonstown, South Africa, that is a story for some other time perhaps.

Although I saw a great deal of my friends we did not talk of our future too much, Roger was the most intelligent of us, and remained in the "A" class while at the Southern, but instead if going on to university, took the civil service entrance exam. and eventually I believe became a tax inspector to farmers in the north of Scotland following his National Service in the RAF, Bert took an engineering apprenticeship with the local authority, and when his time for National Service came round, opted to join the Merchant Navy on a three year commission, what he did after that I have no idea, myself, I was called up into the Royal Marines, and that will be the subject of more writing in the future.

I very much regret not keeping in touch with my friends, and often wonder whether , if they are still living, they to have regrets, we were so close, but new relations are formed, and time, and the world move on, but the one thing that cannot be taken away are the memories of those great years.

You will see that I have enclosed a copy of my penultimate school report, does not make very good reading, only reflects what I said earlier about my lack of concentration during that final year, I do not know whether my final report was any better because I cannot find it, probably not, if the truth be known, I suppose I was absent rather more than would have been hoped, but my migraine problem still manifested itself on occasions, and laid me low often for a few days. I often reflect on my grandchildrens marks on their reports these days, they are so much better, I ask myself, are they working much harder, are the exams easier, or are they being marked more leniently, I rather think that they are working much harder, being as they are, encouraged by their parents with so much enthusiasm, I only wish that I had, had my father looking over my shoulder, and pointing me in the right direction, I may well not have gone to university, but may well have made more use of my time at my wonderful school.

As I said previously, this narrative may well appear disjointed along the way, and I apologise for that, the truth of the matter is, that much of what happened that final year at the Southern, I cannot remember, it matters not now, it just remains for you, my family hopefully to enjoy reading, what to me was an important part of my life.

Epilogue

Whilst writing this, I have experienced every kind of emotion, sometimes quite traumatic, but overall, the trawling of the memory bank, has been an uplifting peering into the past. I have been fortunate over the years in that having grandchildren has allowed me to impart some of what I have written here to them, and at the same time allowing them to make comment, enlightening, to say the least sometimes!

I am sure that as time goes by, I will remember things I should have included, that does not matter now, I truly believe that the overall picture will be seen clearly, that I was someone who though having setbacks along the way, had a wonderful childhood thanks to that year prior to the war when my father was always around, the time with the Webb family, and the influence of my time at the Southern, and at Arnwood with the Davies family. I was never very close to my mother, but she was always around when we returned to Portsmouth after the conflict, she fed, and clothed me, but I never felt that she loved me, perhaps my brothers, and sisters felt the same, I have no way of knowing, I have never been close enough to any of them to find out, families! All this said, blood is thicker than water, and I do care always to know that they keep well.

I have enjoyed writing this somewhat disjointed narrative, and hope that those of you who read it, enjoy the insight into a part of my past, perhaps have a laugh at my expense, and hope that you do not think any the less of me at the end.